Ruckus

A Memoir

Aaron Richard Golub

Library of Congress Cataloguing-in-Publication Data has been applied for

Ruckus: a memoir / Aaron Richard Golub

ALSO BY AARON RICHARD GOLUB

Feisengrad

The Big Cut

SOON TO BE PUBLISHED

Violet Avenue

Dedication

To my son Darrow, my inspiration and my parents, Charles and Esta Golub.

ACKNOWLEDGMENTS

There are those kind of people out there in these tough times. I am fortunate to know George Rush, Phil Cornell, Nick Gage and Sante D'Orazio.

Ruckus owes my longtime friend and masterful editor, George Rush. His loyalty, intellect and perseverance are…what are the synonyms for unmatched?

George introduced me to copy editor and proof reader, Phil Cornell, a man of craftmanship, dedication and sincerity. Check the Epilogue.

Nick's character and great writing has inspired me. He's from Worcester where those qualities are rare. By the way, he gave me the cool idea for the cover.

Cover photo by Sante D'Orazio, artist photographer and creative genius. Nice photo of Darrow or is it me?

TABLE OF CONTENTS

CHAPTER 1:

Worcester is a Real City

Worcester is the place where one starts out in life with nothing and usually ends up with less. It is not unusual for someone who grew up there to introduce themselves by stating, "I'm from Worcester, Mass. Kiss my ass." Worcester is in New England. That explains my phony English accent.

I grew up a second-generation American. My beginnings were humble, a word that never applied to me. My mother Esta's family came from Poland; my father Charles' family from Russia. Their families had settled in Massachusetts just in time to witness two centuries of industrial progress grinding to a halt. The mill town had boomed right after the Second World War. But, in the fifties, textile manufacturing started moving to the South and abroad. Worcester was too close to and too far from Boston. Its population stagnated.

Ripley's Believe It or Not reports that a two-headed "Janus" cat—with two noses and three eyes—lived in Worcester. It went by the names Frank and Louie. I have no reason to doubt it. Worcester is the birthplace of many oddities, born of peculiar experiences which many of us who grew up in Worcester shared. A New York City painter introduced me to Frank Conroy, who wrote an acclaimed memoir, *Stop-Time*. We spent many nights drinking in New York and Nantucket in the '70s. Frank had not written a book in over twenty years. I asked Frank's best friend why. He replied, "In order to write you have to have experiences and Frank hasn't really had any." But Frank was an inspiration to me. His only problem was that he wasn't from Worcester, where unforgettable experiences are unavoidable.

I didn't personally suffer through the decline of the city because, in 1953, I was 11 and a busy boy in grade school. I remember one cold fall day. I was staring at dried leaves chasing the twisting pages of *The Worcester Telegram & Gazette* across the schoolyard's blacktop, near the same gym where the Downbeats played every Friday night. It was morning recess. My friend, Jack Hoffman (Abbie Hoffman's younger brother), was their drummer—a lousy drummer, I heard some kid say, and then he said, "Jack sure can solo!" The icy New England winds made one think of snow, damn snow anytime now, and it snowed like hell in Worcester.

"Hey Golub!"

I hate it when people call me by my last name and here was Steve Krintzman doing it. He was a nice, curly haired, overweight kid whom girls didn't look at twice and with whom I often shot basketball.

"Do you want to go on a hayride tomorrow night?" he asked.

"Go on a *what*?" I answered as the recess bell rang and we moved past the gym's double steel doors. No one had ever told me about hayrides or about girls that went on them.

Then Krintzman said, "We'll go to a farm about ten miles from here in Westboro. We get into a wooden wagon that's pulled by horses, it's full of hay or straw and you're with a bunch of kids in the hay. We go riding around the farm. My mom said it's going to snow. It will be fun."

Fun was the mindless commodity I aimed to acquire every day, a substance everyone seeks, even though it predictably dissipates until none is left.

2

I hardly knew Krintzman, who was a grade ahead. His chubby, round face made him credible, friendly enough to trust in that time when I didn't have any friends. At first, I wondered why he was even talking to me. He was always with a bunch of kids that seemed like "friends" and was very "popular." They called themselves a "clique." Then I started to imagine what a hayride was like. It was a chance to become friends with other kids, even get into their goddamned clique. And I wanted to be popular, but I couldn't figure out the formula. Hell, I was eleven years old, had no friends, and was damn lonely.

I'd spend hours in our attic. I'd put on my train engineer's hat and watch my Lionel locomotive endlessly hauling its boxcars around the track. When I wasn't up there, I'd be in the kitchen fighting with my mother, or at the end of our driveway, playing basketball by myself, trying to shoot the ball through the rusty hoop.

My family had just moved from our tenement apartment, over my dad's store, the Green Street Market, to this leafy paradise where everybody had a front lawn. Mom and the bank paid $21,000 for that two-story brick house at 28 Wamsutta Avenue. It had two white Doric columns framing what was supposed to be a front porch. Most of the money for the house she'd inherited from her father, a successful baker who died of leukemia in the 1940s at age sixty.

Most days you could find me outside in Levi's, a sweatshirt and Converse sneakers—dribbling that basketball until it got too dark to see the backboard.

Then Krintzman said something that would change my life: "Linda Paul is going to be on the hayride."

The name Linda Paul was the sweetest sound I'd ever heard, not exactly "Maria…Maria…Maria" from *West Side Story* but it was my version. Everyone in my neighborhood was an immigrant who had names that sounded like vegetables: Wisniewski, Marano, Glodas, Moustakis,

Zielinski, Blunt. My mother's maiden name was Plevinsky. I despised my last name, Golub, which means pigeon in Russian and was circumcised from Golubovsky. There was suddenly some perfect, shiny pristine phonaesthetics object floating in the clouds, spelled "Linda Paul"—so ethnically pure, simple, and uncomplicated. It didn't have the nauseating sound of goulash in a trash bag.

I told Krintzman, "OK, I'll ask my parents."

I asked my parents about almost everything at that age. I didn't think either one had ever been on a hayride. My mother had been on one or two in the hills of Haverhill, Massachusetts, growing up. My dad's experience was limited to his work at the Green Street Market and his memories of the Second World War. But they said I could go on the hayride.

Friday night came and, around 7, my father drove the grocery store's delivery truck to the farm in Westboro, where I met Krintzman. It was snowing hard, but I was glad. The blizzard made it difficult to see my dad's old truck as these rich kids rolled up in late model four-door Buicks and Cadillacs. Steve was glad to see me and walked me over to a bunch of his friends, who were climbing onto a large horse-drawn, gray wooden wagon. That Krintzman knew his way around, and I wondered why I didn't. My father helped me up the ladder and I tumbled down to the socialization soup of life, into a pile of kids and rough-feeling coarse straw, not hay. It was a straw ride.

As I was getting my bearings, I saw the outline of a girl. Call it mystical crap, but she was like an apparition. It was Linda Paul. She wasted no time introducing herself to me while the other kids were laughing and screaming, throwing straw in each other's faces. I was calm and embarrassed, shy as hell.

"I'm Linda," she smiled. "Steve told me you were coming tonight." I was so infatuated I could hear only her voice trailing off. She was younger than me and was the most beautiful girl I had ever seen, including in movie magazines and on black-and-white TV. She was thin, her hair had small brown curls, and her skin was translucent. I thought I could see through it, all the way to her heart. I was only eleven, goddamnit, and what the f— did I know about being swept up in an emotional typhoon? The feeling was mutual, I told myself.

We didn't even know that the wagon had pulled out under the snowy moon. It didn't take long. We were lying next to each other, locking eyes. Seconds later, there I was kissing her on the lips, my eyes shut tight and my arms squeezing her.

This had to be a dream. Her lips, her hands were so soft. No one in the world had skin like that. Don't ask me how it came to pass that we made out from the moment we met when I didn't know how to make out, never heard about it and I don't think I ever kissed anyone before that, not even members of my own family, not even the wall or a pet.

The night ended at 9 p.m. My dad picked me up in our Chevrolet truck. Linda's mother, Helen, glared at me as her daughter climbed into the back seat of their new, black-and-white, four-door Buick Roadmaster.

The hayride was over—except now I was in love with Linda Paul and had her phone number memorized. Her parents had a different number. In the Worcester telephone directory, two numbers were listed under Morris Paul, 15 Kensington Road; the second one was the Children's Phone, Swift-1069. Rich kids had their own phones in their rooms. Kensington (a district, in a royal borough, in London) is an English surname that was an area in England used to designate royal hunting grounds. No wonder I felt like a serf. This was the first and last hayride I would ever go on, with or without her.

After school on Monday, I rang Linda at her Kensington quarters. Her mother picked up.

"Hi, is Linda there?" I asked, nervous as hell.

"Who is this?" The chill breezed through the receiver. Does anyone really want to admit who they are in such a moment?

"Richard Golub," I answered, not brimming with confidence.

"No," she ruled, like an angry judge. Then: *click.*

She had to be lying. Or maybe she made a mistake. Either way, I was frozen, afraid to redial the number. The telephone is a barrier that is not easily overcome by dialing. I felt *crestfallen.* I found that adjective in my *Word Wealth* book, a volume I took wherever I went. I was constantly finding new words and searching definitions. That word perfectly described my feelings, the plummet from the hayride high to the nasty encounter with Linda's coldhearted mother. I propped myself up saying, "So what, someday she'll be dead."

I had never encountered an adult who acted that way. Older people were always pinching my cheeks and telling me how adorable I was. Like they tell every kid. My father's mother, Ida Golub, who was married three times, said I was her favorite of ten grandchildren, so she must have known a good thing when she saw it. I always knew I had her support and trust, which I carry with me to this day.

"Linda will never call me back"—those words repeated themselves over and over in my head. Repetition was a classic Golub syndrome. My brain just worked that way, although it could be damn monotonous. I forgave my shortcomings because that was simply the way I was. I equated my behavior with the rest of humanity. I ground my teeth, therefore, probably everyone ground their teeth.

Between hooping a few outside on the b-ball court after school, I tried to see Linda. It was hard and she was usually not available. It began to sink in that the Pauls would never understand me or my family.

I tried to talk with my mother about what happened, which was intense and rocky because my mother was a difficult, complex character. Everything I did interfaced with her life, stenciled with her childhood spent working fourteen hours a day in her father's bakery and with the stark loneliness of wondering whether my dad would return alive from the Second World War.

Later in the kitchen, where we held all our family summits, I spoke to my mother. She was cooking and, as usual, complaining about what a bitch it was to cook. You had to talk to her back while she was gazing into the oven at the dish she'd just scorched to a crisp—that'd be breakfast, lunch, or dinner—accompanied by her burnt analysis of my problems.

She asked, "So, have you heard from Linda?"

She sounded like she knew all about Linda and they had some secret coded friendship. After all, it was just another woman. I didn't tell my mother that I heard guys in Worcester said girls like Linda were "unattainable."

"No, Ma, after the hayride I couldn't reach her on the phone and left a message with her mother."

I picked away at one of my mother's blackened pancakes and took a sip of boiling hot chocolate. She wanted the relationship to work out—even at this nascent stage. But how could she help? She'd have a better shot at contacting the Dalai Lama, in Tibet, than getting Helen Paul's attention.

"Helen Paul," my mother huffed. "A real snob. Sometimes I see her downtown shopping. Never talks to anyone, very ritzy-titzy in her mink coat. A few years back she worked as a secretary for Paul Hats, that big factory at the corner of Park Avenue and Chandler Streets. Then she snagged the boss, Linda's father, Morris. Got him to get a divorce. He's much older than her. Some people say he is a nice guy, but she is tough as nails."

I later learned that Morris was a recent arrival in America from Europe. The French might call him an *arriviste*. He'd changed his last name, as we did. I don't know where Helen came from, but my mother was right about her being tough as nails. That phone call was deadly painful.

I was in love in, of all places, the town where Valentine's Day cards origi-
nated in America in 1847. Cupid's arrow shot straight into my heart.

I didn't want to risk the possible embarrassment of calling again and
having Helen hang up on me. Or Linda answering, telling me she couldn't
talk, and then having to wait forever for her to call. The shitty possibilities
were endless. I couldn't see her face to face because we went to different
grade schools, or what they called middle schools. I went to May Street,
and she went to Midland Street. I had that lonely sensation that we'd never
see each other again.

* * *

On weekends, I watched a lot of movies to distract myself from Linda.
Movie stars were my heroes. Kirk Douglas shot to the top of my list when I
saw him in *Spartacus*. I thought he was the strongest man who ever lived.
He could talk without moving his lips—and even his lips had muscles.

After school, I stuck to my routine: supervising my electric trains in
the attic and playing basketball. I also hung around with some neighborhood kids who were fun but a poor substitute for Linda.

Tony and Johnnie Solitro were twins—wild, a little looney, but
good-natured. They laughed at everything and everyone, until their
mother hollered them home for dinner with her high-pitched voice.

The Toomeys lived two doors down in a big Colonial white house
that had a stairway right in the middle. Would you believe they had a professional bowling alley in the basement? That impressed me. It was grand
to walk in the front door and see rooms on both sides of the staircase. I
may have seen that in a Gregory Peck movie, but I didn't tell the Toomeys
that candlepin bowling was invented in Worcester in 1879.

Old man Robert Toomey had a factory on Plantation Street called
Robert J. Toomey Co. Clerical Apparel. It made *vestments*, which my *Word
Wealth* said meant religious clothing. Toomey called them "comfort shirts."

The Toomeys had four daughters and one son. His name was Stanley. He was a little off. Stanley was short, scrawny, and used to run around biting his calloused right hand, screaming "I-K-E-E." Perhaps he meant Ike, nickname of our newly elected president, Dwight D. Eisenhower. Stanley frequently called me Mrs. White. Somehow, he confused me with my mother's best friend, Sarah White, known as "Sahara Gobi," at my house, where she regularly gossiped at our kitchen table. She was infamous for walking around the neighborhood at 7 a.m., in her tattered nightgown and ragged cloth house slippers, smoking a Camel or a Lucky. Anyway, I called Stanley "Stan the Man," even though he in no way resembled baseball Hall of Famer Stan Musial. Stanley would often appear, unexpectedly, at our front door, ring the bell, and ask me with a flourish, *"Hors d'oeuvres, monsieur?"* He didn't have any *hors d'oeuvres* and I have no idea where he learned these two words of French. No one in Worcester spoke French.

Back then, kids would call each other "retard" or say "you're mental" anytime someone did something silly. But several of our neighbors had mentally ill children. That didn't stop us from playing with them and having fun. Across the street, at the end of a field, there was the Daniels house. They had a son named Daniel probably because they couldn't think of a first name better than their last name. He, too, had mental problems. He was a large kid whose development was stuck at fourteen years old. He was over six feet tall and must have weighed 200 pounds. He'd pick up sewer covers, pressing them over his head, claiming: "I'm the strongest man in the world!" One time he collapsed, and firemen had to remove a steel manhole cover from his chest.

Then there was Pericles (Perry) Eliopolis. Perry was an enigma (*enigma* being one of my first *Word Wealth* discoveries, though I rarely used it, preferring to keep the word out on the terrace). I knew next to nothing about Perry, other than that he was about two years older than me. And huge. He often walked around without a shirt, displaying his strapping arms and chest. He looked like a Grecian sculpture, so we called him the

Golden Greek. Unlike his namesake, he was not an orator. He never called anyone by their name or looked you in the eye. But, like Toomey, Daniels, and the Solitro brothers, he radiated spirit. That's why we were all friends.

On any given day Perry would be roaming the streets, like an escaped ape, looking for trouble. One hot summer day in 1959, when Perry's mind was dialing the wrong number, he planted himself in the middle of the intersection of June and Chandler. Motorists stopped, not wanting to run over a boy. Perry walked up to them and told them to pop their car hoods. Cowed by his size, they obeyed. Perry then lifted their hoods and removed their distributor caps, causing their engines to stall. The crippled cars set off a domino traffic jam that went back to Newton Square. When the cops finally showed up, they asked Perry why he did it.

"I didn't do nuthin'," he insisted.

That was the standard Worcester denial. It wasn't a lie so much as a belief that whatever you did didn't amount to anything.

Near my house, on a high hill on May Street, was a mental hospital. It was called Fairlawn. It was once part of the estate of a rich guy. It looked haunted and sinister, but who cared? Every so often, the Solitro Brothers, Dan Daniels, Stanley Toomey, and I would put on our Davy Crockett coonskin caps and head up to Fairlawn to play cards with the inmates when the caretakers were on break. There were no game boards at the asylum, not even a Monopoly board or a deck of cards. So, we'd sneak into the kitchen, find loaves of raisin bread, and round up three or four inmates. We'd use raisin bread slices as cards and play raisin-stakes poker. We'd sit there for a minute, scrutinizing our raisins. Then one of us would scream out, "Full house!" or "Straight flush!" The inmates usually folded. When Stanley would ask me, "How can you tell one slice from another?" I'd always reply, "Shut up and play!"

* * *

One of the scarier kids in the neighborhood was Red Turner, who lived on September Street. He was a large boy with carrot-colored hair. One day he appeared on our front lawn swinging an ax over his head. He was babbling, "Kill! Kill! Kill!" My father marched right up to Red and grabbed the ax.

My dad was braver than I knew at the time. Over the years, I learned about his heroism in the Second World War. In Italy, his unit, the 36th Infantry, fought the retreating Germans through the bloody battles of Monte Cassino, Anzio, and the Rapido River. Shortly after the Allies took Rome, my dad was directing military traffic in Trastevere, a neighborhood where Roman Jews had been in hiding. A five-year-old girl and her father approached him and asked if he had any food. He gave them some K-rations. Her father, Elio Polaco, noticed my dad's Star of David medallion worn around his neck and asked if he would like to worship with them. He guided my father to Tempio Maggiore di Roma, where hundreds of Roman Jews were waiting outside. Breaking the wax seals on its doors, my dad entered with the rest of the Jews. Inside, he was given the honor of delivering the Hebrew blessing over the liberation of Rome. That synagogue now has two plaques. One is dedicated to Victor Emmanuel II, the last king of Italy. The other is in "Memory of Charles Aaron Golub, the First American Jewish Soldier Who Entered This Synagogue and Prayed to Celebrate the Liberation of Rome—June 4, 1944."

That same year, about a month later, my father was on patrol in Strasbourg, France, when a German shell blew up the farmhouse where my dad's unit was hiding from a Nazi tank battalion. He lay unconscious in a ditch for two days. Finally, he woke up and discovered that both his legs were broken. There was a full moon out and, seeing two soldiers smoking nearby, he was about to yell to them for help. Just then, he heard them speaking German. He rolled back into the ditch. When the Germans left, he began crawling back toward the Allied lines—following the North Star. Miles later, some G.I.'s found him. A Catholic chaplain gave him last rites on the hood of a jeep.

But he pulled through. I was three when Dad came back to Worcester. My mother took a picture of me with him in his dress uniform. I can still feel his hand. Once, when we were eating, a small shard of shrapnel fell out of his eye. I used to stare at the long scars on his back. Rarely did my dad have a conversation that didn't remind him of a day in the war.

* * *

But life went on. A few months had passed since the hayride, and I still hadn't heard from Linda. Whenever I asked Krintzman about her, I got the stock answer: "I don't know anything, haven't seen her."

That was a lie. He liked her, too, and wasn't going to give me an edge or an answer. We all reluctantly accept bullshit, but I was getting irritated. Around the beginning of 1954, I made it my business to call her again. This time she answered. I was nervous, trying to get the conversation going in a cool way when ordinary words would have done fine. Trying to be witty and smart doesn't always work. Women like ordinary stuff.

"Hello," she said.

"Hi," I managed to say. "Richard."

"Richard who?"

She didn't know it was me. I was forced to say my last name, something I never liked to do. But maybe she knew a lot of Richards, so I excused her.

"Golub," I confessed, not knowing how to pronounce my last name. Was it "Go-lub?" Or "Gol—ub?"

"Oh, Richie!" she said. "The boy from the hayride?"

Her cold question informed me she was a ball-breaker in training. This wasn't a good sign, and I should have hung up right there and then. I would've saved myself years of heartache.

"That's me, do you want to go for a walk?" When you don't drive, and you're twelve years old, you ask girls to go for a walk, although lots of the pretty ones didn't like to walk.

"Yes, that would be all right," she said, "but I must be home for dinner at 5:30. I live on Kensington Road, number 15. Do you know where that is, off Pleasant Street?"

"Yes," I answered.

I hadn't a clue where 15 Kensington was. I figured I'd ask my mother to drop me off on the corner and I would walk there nonchalantly, acting as if I didn't have parents who delivered me.

Luckily, my thirty-five-year-old mother did just that without asking any questions—not even expecting me to comment that I must really like this girl and that it was the first time I had a "date." My mother was in one of her alternating moods and this was the good side, the good mom.

I walked up the hill and went to the front door, intimidated right up to ringing the bell. Shit, I was very nervous and couldn't calm down. The chimes were so loud, even *they* embarrassed me. I thought I had awakened her entire family. Then the door opened. A tall, imposing figure with translucent skin, just like Linda's, stood in the doorway. It had to be her older brother, Richie Paul. A real prick of the first order.

"Who are *you*?" he sneered.

I didn't know what I'd done to make him angry, other than to come calling on his sister. But he was very pissed. I peered behind him and saw a pink-walled living room with some nice furniture. I wanted to go in because I liked her and they had a center stairway, much grander even than the Toomeys'.

"Richard," I said, introducing myself. "Richard Golub. I came to see Linda."

13

I could barely get the words out of my mouth. He scared the shit out of me. I thought he was going to slam the door in my face. Everything felt funny, even my new clothes seemed dirty and I didn't know who I was. I must have looked self-conscious and ugly. Adults in Worcester told kids to "Be yourself." That was a good one that kept me constantly looking for myself. Whatever I had done in my short life, I didn't deserve this asshole. Like my dad said, I was a "happy go-lucky kid" and was nice to everyone. Who the fuck was this intermeddler?

"Hey, is Richard at the door?" I heard her ask from upstairs.

Help was on the way.

"There is an asshole down here," Richie Paul boomed before walking away from the door. He made me feel I was the hole in someone's ass—something I'd never felt before. But now I was *in,* and I sat on a rose-colored armchair that was like nothing in our house. The lights in the living room were not on but it was still daylight, and the shades were half opened. Plus, the Pauls had drapes, just like in a Lana Turner movie. I could tell that they didn't use this room very often. Like most people in Worcester with living rooms, the Pauls didn't live in theirs. It was for guests.

About fifteen minutes went by before Linda came down and formally greeted me, like I was a friend of a friend, not the kid she repeatedly French-kissed on the hayride. And as a point of information, she French'd me, not the other way around. Where did this phony shit come from?

She immediately apologized for her brother—he went to Worcester Academy, a posh private school—she swore he was a great guy and that she loved him immensely.

"He doesn't like boys coming over to the house to see me," she said, pulling a navy-blue cardigan sweater over her white-collared blouse while we walked out the front door. It made me wonder how many boys like me came to see her. Maybe her musical name—*Linda Paul*—had entranced them and they were lining up around the block. She was getting me on track without wasting any time. Jealousy swept through me for the first time. It would return many times.

We walked down the hill and around the corner onto Pleasant Street—not too far and not saying very much. It was probably my fault because I can easily be like my father, who was gentle, easygoing, and quiet. In fact, I have none of those qualities now. Sometimes when I'm with a beautiful woman, I tend to go dead silent, talk myself into a corner, or just sound insane. When my father took my mother out for the first time, he didn't say a word until he drove her home after the movies. Before she got out of the car, he asked her out again. "Goddamnit," she snapped. "You didn't say a word all night, I don't even know who you are, and you want to do this all over again?" They got married three months later and stayed together for sixty-one years.

"I would like to see you this Saturday," I said.

"That isn't possible," she replied. "Every Saturday we go to our club."

She was talking about the Mount Pleasant Country Club, the exclusive domain of well-off Jews who'd been excluded from gentile clubs.

Linda went on, "I play golf with my mother and father, and we have lunch."

"Golf?" I asked casually. "I've seen that in newspapers, on the sports page. I've never played."

The truth was I'd never seen it played, or seen it on the sports page, or any other place. But I knew that people who were rich played golf and tennis, sports that required a ball to be hit with some instrument. They wore special clothes that helped them hit the ball hard and far.

"I can't invite you to the club," she apologized. "My mother wouldn't let me invite you."

"What is a club?" I asked.

I was dying for her explanation since I didn't have any friends and a club sounded like a place where you could get a bunch of them.

"When we go there we eat lunch, sometimes dinner, in the dining room. My father drinks a cocktail with my mother, and I have a Shirley Temple."

"You mean you drink the actress?"

"No, silly, that is the name of a kid's drink."

"Oh."

I still had no idea what was in a Shirley Temple. Moxie was my most exotic beverage, straight out of the Green Street Market cooler.

"Would you like to go back to my house?" she asked. "I could show you some of my paintings."

In my house there were no paintings, just wallpaper. We didn't even have any books, except for my mother's twelfth grade history book from Haverhill High School, her yearbook, *The Thinker* (with Rodin's sculpture embossed on the cover), and a Hebrew prayer book.

We slipped back into Linda's house by way of the kitchen, where her mother was talking on the phone, down to the brightly lit, knotty pine finished basement. Almost all rich people in Worcester had knotty pine finished basements and drove Cadillacs—or four-door Buicks if they wanted to be lower key. They always seemed to get richer in times of adversity and suffered little of life's ill-fated events. Money just went to money, confirming the Italian expression that "It always rains on the floor that is already wet." Linda took me over to the corner where there was an unfinished painting sitting on an easel. She said to me, "What do you think?"

I wasn't thinking, I was getting hot.

"Think of what?" I was confused and not exactly a member of the National Gallery.

"The painting. Do you think it is beautiful? I painted it. That's a landscape."

No one had ever asked for my artistic critique before. We didn't talk that way around my house. What the hell was a landscape?

"What do you mean by 'beautiful'?" I asked.

I couldn't help myself. The words just popped out. I felt self-conscious, as they said in the fifties.

"Can't you see the colors? The yellow with the blue? They go perfectly together."

Was she saying I was stupid? If she wasn't saying that, maybe feeling dumb was an intrinsic step in falling in love. Maybe I was being subverted—brainwashed—by someone I believed had superior knowledge, who lived in a superior house and who maybe was superior.

"I can see the green trees, the blue sky," I said, not having a clue about what I was looking at. "It is very good to look at. It looks good."

At the same time, I said to myself I could look out the window, if we weren't in the basement, and see the same things. That was the best I could come up with, and it was all right for the moment because she came over to me, took me by the hand, and moved me across the room as if I were a piece of furniture. There was a record player with a 45 rpm of "Stranger in Paradise," Tony Bennett's version. Linda lifted the turntable's tonearm and placed the needle on the vinyl. She took me to the middle of the room, wrapped her arm around my neck, and kissed me softly on the lips. We started dancing. Both of us got very hot. These finished basements were the place to get a girl "hot." That was what we called a girl when she was ready to have sex—she was hot. Guys would get "hot," too. Or so I heard.

The way she wrapped her arm around my neck, hayride style, was ethereal. We were in a special, comfortable, private world that no one else could enter. It felt so natural, as if we'd done this a thousand times. I closed my eyes, my temperature was rising and we floated into outer space, like they said in the fifties. There is no way to duplicate those feelings and I knew, even then, that I was already losing her. It was just too good to be true. For the life of me, I wanted to hold on, never let her go off that basement floor, because when the music was over she'd be that much closer to leaving me. Maybe it was because her monster goddamn brother and ogre mother were upstairs thinking about how to pry her loose from me, or maybe that's just the way things are when you want them too much. What the hell did her family know about getting hot anyway? They couldn't get hot if they were sitting on a stove.

CHAPTER 2:

Into the Arts

It wasn't till much later that I found out I wasn't the only one Linda wrapped her arms around in that basement. There were other guys who entered during the short periods when we broke up, and even while we were together. Some of them told me that I was "the real love of her life." Of course, that news was not comforting because it was way too late to backtrack.

When I think about that day she sprung the word "beautiful" on me, I don't know why I didn't tell her that I wasn't exactly a stranger to culture. Shit, I played the piano for three years, until I was eleven. No goddamn *Chopsticks* either! I performed Classical! On Saturdays, I studied with Madelyn Sadick, at the Day Building on Main Street. She inspired me. When I walked down the painted red corridor to her studio, I thought of nothing but flats and sharps. She gave me yellow-bound selections from Schirmer's Library of Musical Classics to practice. Every day, I played Beethoven, Brahms, and Liszt on the rented, upright piano, in our dining room. I was very capable at painfully curling my fingers. Even my mother, in one of her thirty or so good moods, said, "Rich, you can really tickle the ivories!"

I wanted to play well. When I messed up, Ms. Sadick gently held my hands and showed me the correct way. Every time I performed a composition well, she awarded me a small, white, marble-dust statue of a famous composer. I had over twenty of those busts on my upright piano. They were my prized collection. Then one day, my mother rushed into the dining room, screaming at me for something I didn't do. Her arm swept the entire group of my cherished composers onto the floor. One by one they shattered, and so did I, as they disintegrated into specks of white powder.

After that I wouldn't—couldn't—play the piano. I was traumatized. An artist girlfriend I had later in life told me her father was once so pissed at her that he destroyed all her paintings and sketches. My mother pressed me to return to the keyboard, but she never apologized for what she'd done. The only way I could get out of piano was to promise her I would play another instrument. I chose the clarinet. Even now, I wonder how I came up with a wind instrument, especially one that required a wet reed. But the clarinet was portable, so I didn't have to practice it in front of her.

My clarinet teacher was Mr. Thayer. His studio was also in the Day Building. I went there every Wednesday, at 5:30 p.m., by myself. They turned the lights off at 5 p.m. and, during the winter when it got dark early, the Day Building was frightening. It had a squeaky elevator whose iron cage let you see the cab floating up and down the shadowy shaft. I felt like I was being hoisted to the gallows as it creaked toward Thayer's studio on the fourth floor. Thayer looked and sounded like Boris Karloff. I felt like I was learning clarinet in the *House of Wax*, which came out in 3D that year. It was tortuous—the music lesson, that is. I felt lucky to get out of there alive.

By the time I met Linda I'd kind of lost interest in music. I didn't tell her I'd been an accomplished pianist. Maybe I could have played her something "beautiful" if I'd practiced again. The Pauls didn't know shit about Brahms, Beethoven, or Liszt. I also thought it wise not to mention the musical sideline of my dad and Uncle Izzie, who sang country and western songs every Wednesday, on WORC, to advertise their grocery store. "Green Street Market has the ham and the lamb," they'd sing. "Steaks or roasts or even chops, you'll find Green Street Market tops!" Print ads for the show depicted the Golub brothers in long beards, looking like the cough drop-making Smith Brothers. There was no way I was going to tell Linda or her family about the *Itsy Golub Show*.

After our make-out session in her knotty pine rec room, Linda and I went out steadily for a couple of years. She never agreed to "go steady" officially. She wouldn't accept my engraved sterling silver ID bracelet. We would talk on the phone for hours. My mother wanted to meet her, but I didn't want my mom getting involved. I dreaded the inevitable comparison with Linda's mother, who dressed much better. I did become a regular visitor at the Pauls' home, though I was restricted to the living room. Only once did they offer me food. It was a Sunday morning. The Pauls were in the dining room feasting on smoked salmon, sturgeon, and herring; bagels and bialys; plus, cream cheese, onions, tomatoes, and capers. I sat in my parlor cell, listening to them gorge themselves. Finally, Linda's jovial father paid me a visit. He presented me with a plate that held a single black olive.

"Would you like to try an olive?" he asked. "They're very good."

I so wanted to shove that olive up his ass. But I ate it.

Whenever her family belittled me, Linda and I would try to escape. We usually went out walking in the neighborhood, holding hands, talking about what we were going to do with our lives. We never spoke about us being together in the future.

The future was set for her. She already owned stocks and bonds. Linda was going to move to New York City and become a famous artist who lived in Greenwich Village. Maybe she would hang out with Jackson Pollock, Robert Rauschenberg, and Jasper Johns, possibly move to The Springs, swim in the Atlantic, and buy mackerel in Montauk.

At least once a month, Linda's family drove down to New York City, stayed at the Plaza Hotel, went shopping for cashmere anything, went to fancy restaurants, and attended the theater. The Pauls had relatives on Park Avenue who acted just like the Worcester Pauls. Like her father, Linda's uncle was a milliner, which was a big business back then. In those days, every woman wore a black hat with a veil or some artificial fruit or fake flowers on top of their other hats.

Worcester ladies wore long black gloves. There was no pronounced feminist movement then, but women there were firmly in control. Eleven-year-old Linda had the upper hand, starting with that hayride. My goddess could achieve anything she chose. She referred to herself as a painter from Day One to the last time I saw her. I found her very *sophisticated*—a word I learned from her. Which was rare, because usually words were *my* currency.

I admit the Pauls pissed me off with their wealth. But I had my *Word Wealth*—that little blue book I read every day. Since we didn't have much money, I figured if I knew enough words, and if I could put those words in the right order, I could convince Worcester folks and other people to give me money. That's how I would make a living. That's how I would get rich. That's what lawyers did in Worcester—they talked. Slowly I became convinced that I wanted to be a lawyer. Lawyers were respected, and they were paid for their words.

So, I learned to pronounce words like *contiguous, approbation, ingenuous, didactic* and many more that could be used to persuade. I also memorized definitions. A *nonagon* was a nine-sided figure. I dropped *nonagon* whenever the occasion called for it. Instead of reciting poetry or singing show tunes, I would peel off "$100 words." That's what people called them. I would tell my relatives and acquaintances stories heavily peppered with my latest discoveries. For example, we lived next to the Pemsteins. The father, Bernard "Bunny" Pemstein, was a *disingenuous* man with three kids and a wife. Don't ask me why people called him "Bunny." It may have been because of his childlike quality, but he also looked like a rabbit. Bunny was married to Zelda Pemstein, an enormous, chirpy woman who wore long plum-colored skirts. Bunny could be *didactic,* but he and I had a *rapport,* I would say. I could talk to him more easily than I could with my dad. We had important things in common—such as dirty jokes and our shared *obsession* with Anita Ekberg and Lana Turner.

Around this time, one of my heroes, James Dean, was killed in a car crash. His death was hard on me because I, too, considered myself a rebel. My other interests, when I wasn't playing basketball or thinking about Linda, were reading ("The Hardy Boys," comic books) and watching professional sports in the basement. The Cleveland Browns were my team; my heroes were Otto Graham and Tank Younger. I was also a rabid baseball fan. Even though we lived in the heart of Massachusetts, I didn't give a damn about the Boston Red Sox. The Yankees—with Casey Stengel at the helm—were foremost in my mind. As the years went by, I became a bigger and bigger Yankees fan. I couldn't get enough of Yogi Berra, Mickey Mantle, Hank Bauer, Whitey Ford, and Don Larsen. But I knew all the teams and players. I would spend hours upon hours playing with Topps Major League Baseball cards and chewing Topps bubble gum until I couldn't move my jaw.

We played a couple of games with our cards. "Flipping" was where you and your friend tossed your cards toward the ground, with the objective of making them land face-up. The winner got to keep the other guy's card. I loved flinging one card after another at a target. This was also known as "scaling." Sitting on a toilet seat, I could launch a card through a towel rack and into a soap dish. One of the hardest scaling feats was tossing a card so it landed just so, leaning against a wall. I could "lean" baseball cards from ten feet away. I didn't tell anyone my secret: It was in the wrist. There was no place I couldn't scale a baseball card. Kids said I was a world-class card-thrower. I would scale Ralph Kiner, Mickey Mantle, Yogi Berra, Hank Bauer, and other famous players across streets, over fences, into windows, and onto roofs with blazing accuracy. Ricky Jay, the famous sleight-of-hand artist, who could fling a playing card into a watermelon, had nothing on me. I often daydreamed about becoming a professional card-thrower. I could be on *The Ed Sullivan Show*—scaling cards across a stage to the delight of millions of dumbfounded Americans.

Linda never knew about this talent, which was also artistic. My cards spoke to me. I confided in them because they were my friends, until I had human ones. Can you imagine what Linda's mother and brother would have said about my cards and me in the bathroom all afternoon? It would've been too weird.

I didn't think about any other girl. There were many days when I thought of her that I got sick to my stomach. Although she really liked me, she said her parents restricted the times and places we could see one another. We still danced in her basement, with the lights off, to "Stranger in Paradise." We still made out furiously. Sometimes, if I was feeling bold, I dared to touch her tits.

* * *

Meanwhile, I was learning to fight. We'd come from a rough neighborhood. There were bars up and down Green Street. I used to deliver deli sandwiches to the players in the twenty-four-hour poker game in the back of The Casablanca, Jigger McGrail's dance hall, where prostitutes foxtrotted with rummies. Sometimes, when winos couldn't afford booze, they'd come into our store and ask for hot peppers and Woolite as a substitute. Guys would box on the street. They'd put a dime into a parking meter; when its red flag popped up, the "round" was over. My father wouldn't let me deliver to The White Eagle, aka the Polish and American Club (the P&A), because its customers would get so revved up watching Friday night boxing on TV that they'd get into their own vicious bouts. A victor would sometimes roll the unconscious loser into the middle of Green Street in the hope that a passing car might finish the vanquished.

We'd moved to the tree-lined West Side, a good part of Worcester. But my "classy" neighborhood provided no refuge from bullies. On any given day, I could be in class at May Street School and one of the tough kids would come up to me and say, "One o'clock today!" That meant I would have to fight one of them at the end of Marcy Street. It was a dirt road near my house but still too far to run home. For the rest of the morning, I would shit my pants knowing I was going to get punched in the mouth at 1 p.m. I'd be put in a headlock, my face turning crimson, while another kid shouted, "Golub, you asshole, do you give up?"

Although I was afraid, I didn't chicken out of these fights. Well ... except if I was due to fight Rick Gilbert, the toughest kid in school. Some days I would try to sneak down May Street to avoid the inevitable pandemonium at the Marcy boxing ring. It was no different during medieval times, when one traveled in the countryside fearing highwaymen who would rob and kill you. When I got to the top of May Street, I would try to run all the way home. Usually, a couple of Rick Gilbert's pals would spot me and escort me to the fight. Sometimes, I'd try to evade them by cutting through backyards to get home. But Gilbert's gang always found my shortcut and waited for me behind trees and bushes. Kids all over Worcester were doing the same thing to avoid some tough Irish or Italian or Greek kid waiting on the corner to bloody their face. This was our Cold War.

My most memorable incident occurred in the fifth grade.

Jimmy McBride was a freckled-faced, thin kid who was strong and tough. He picked on me every day. One day, during recess, I went to the boy's room on the fourth floor. Spying McBride beneath me in the schoolyard, I opened the bathroom's ripple glass window, climbed onto the sill, unzipped my fly, and aimed my pecker. Remembering the bathroom graffiti that "soldiers with short muskets must stand closer to the firing line," I tried to piss on him.

Classmates below recognized my cotton powder-blue pants. They saw my pecker. They shouted like a church choir, "There's Golub, pissing!"

I stood there like a fountain in a Greek sculpture garden as I gave that fucking bully a moral adjustment. The crafty Jimmy McBride jumped out the way, but my fifth-grade teacher, Miss Michelle, did not. My piss drenched her brunette hair and her red cloth coat that had large, black brass buttons. When she looked up, she caught it in the face.

A janitor walked into the bathroom and caught me on the window-sill. He grabbed me by the ear and dragged me to the principal's office.

Mary Ellen Shea, the white-haired principal, screamed at me at the top of her lungs. She said I was rotten to the core. I offered no rebuttal about McBride and what he'd done to me. She proceeded to kick me out of school. I walked home and found my apron-clad mother hanging laundry on our four-sided clothesline in the backyard. I told her what happened. Curiously, she didn't get that angry. She'd already heard from Shea. My mother said that no one had ever done anything like this in her lifetime. I think my behavior must have given her a kind of nervous breakdown, because smaller infractions had caused her to bounce much farther off the wall. I believe my assassination attempt was so offbeat and cool that it went into a space in her brain labeled "to be figured out, if ever, much later." Frankly, I still can't sort it out. Days before, I'd scoped out my fourth-floor bathroom sniper perch like Lee Harvey Oswald did when he shot JFK from the sixth floor of the Texas School Book Depository. What had I been thinking?

Shea allowed me to come back after three days. I had to go to her office, show remorse, and write an apology to Miss Michelle. It didn't end there. When I finished sixth grade, rather than getting a diploma, I received an unheard-of rolled-up Certificate of Attendance. Some kid in my class said I could wipe my ass with my certificate because it was useless.

I never told Linda about the incident, but everyone else in town seemed to know. To this day, whenever I meet someone from Worcester, it's the first thing they bring up. It's a great success reducer. In 2000, when *The New York Times* interviewed me about my life and career, the reporter said she'd heard I had peed out a window in grade school. My urine was reported in the paper of record's "Public Lives" column. No one else can lay claim to that distinction.

My expulsion from May Street School was the first of many establishments from which, I am proud to say, I've been booted over the decades.

Despite being deprived of a diploma, I attended May Street's graduation ceremony in a rented cap and gown. In the fall, I hoped for a fresh start at Chandler Junior High, a brand-new white brick school that looked like a huge one-story Richard Neutra house. The principal's name was John Corcoran. He was a towering man, about fifty-five. He wore dark brown gabardine suits and took enormous pride in his highly polished shoes and his gleaming bald head. Everyone suspected he was shining his shoes and his head with the same product. But his secretary told one of the students that Corcoran kept a dedicated can of head wax in his top drawer. The students called him "Chrome Dome." When he walked around the corridors, the kids would say, "The sun is out."

Corcoran was a prick who really enjoyed the expulsion process. Outside his office was a long, splintery oak bench, usually occupied by three or four sullen kids who had been sent to see the principal for swearing, throwing paper airplanes, not returning from the boy's room, acting wise to a teacher, playing cards, or any of a million other violations of minor, childish insubordination, which I gladly committed at one time or another. Soon thereafter, these kids found themselves walking on Chandler Street during school hours, kicked out by Chrome Dome. You were nobody at Chandler until you'd been "expelled." I was in Chrome Dome's office nearly every week. I bragged that I'd been "bounced out" more times than anyone else—enjoying the mental picture of my ass bouncing down May Street to my home.

My insubordination wasn't confined to Chandler. Every Sunday, I went to Hebrew School at the Beth Israel Synagogue. My goal was my bar mitzvah— becoming a man—a milestone for any Jewish boy. But I found memorizing the Torah tedious, so I always pretended I needed to go to the bathroom. Every ten minutes, I raised my hand. My teacher must have thought I had the prostate of a seventy-five-year-old man.

I suffered so much in those classes that my mom hired a private tutor, Rabbi Steinberg. He was a short man with small, soft hands. He wore dark suits and a wide-brimmed, black fedora. Every Thursday, at 4 o'clock, we'd sit in the dining room and read Hebrew. It was hard because Rabbi Steinberg's breath smelled like aged Porterhouse. I dreaded Thursdays, when "the old steak" would soon be breathing in my face for an hour. Even now I think about how awful Thursday might smell.

Despite this rabbinical halitosis, I started picking up Hebrew. I was about two months away from my bar mitzvah and doing well when the doorbell rang during one of my lessons. My mother answered it. There stood my former principal, Mary Ellen Shea, looking like she wanted to murder someone, namely Richard Golub. Rabbi Steinberg and I went to the screen door and listened as Miss Shea screamed, "Look at my car! Just look at my car!" Her white Buick Special was parked in front of our house. On the driver's side someone had written in red lipstick: "MISS SHEA IS A FUCKING ASSHOLE. [Signed] RICHARD GOLUB."

I was in shock, although I believed the statement to be accurate: You had to be an asshole to drive around in a car proclaiming you as an asshole. It was almost Talmudic. Even though I thought Miss Shea was a fucking asshole, I didn't write that on her car. It couldn't be my handwriting—the penmanship was excellent.

Rabbi Steinberg, practically choking, looked accusingly at me. My mother was angry but not at me.

"That isn't Richie's handwriting, and he didn't do it," she told Miss Shea. "He has been home with me all day. He is in the middle of his Hebrew lesson."

Miss Shea had already chucked me out of May Street, but I was now at Chandler and out of her jurisdiction. Nevertheless, she had called the cops. They soon arrived and wanted to interrogate me down at the station. I was up for it because I love questions. But the crime was quickly resolved. Two girls, who lived across the street, pled guilty when they saw the police car. One of them was a girl named Paula. I thought I'd recognized her handwriting. Later, when things blew over, I told Paula she should have printed.

* * *

As a school, Chandler did have certain advantages. My chief tormentor, Rick Gilbert, didn't go there, and my first real friend, Arthur Freedman, did.

Arthur and I were both in Hebrew School. I didn't really know him then, except that we both screamed in the hallways, at the same time, and did our best to pester mean Mr. Plitch, the school administrator, whose name, we were sure to remind everyone, rhymed with bitch. We didn't miss that joke.

Meeting Arthur was a turning point in my life. I'd always been a little wild but, fundamentally, I was morally pure. Arthur? He really knew the ropes. He was wise beyond his years. He had tons of evil charisma. He could get anyone to do anything. To this day, I don't know how he became so savvy. He introduced me to swimming naked at the YMCA (commenting on the wrinkled asses of the older Y members in the shower), fishing in a polluted lake, playing cards for money, wearing tight Levi's and white T-shirts, smoking unfiltered Marlboros, shoplifting at the five-and-dime, jerking off, and swearing like an army sergeant. No wonder we called him "Dirty Art."

From the time I met Dirty Art, to the last time we spoke, in 2021, his answer to most questions was "Arbo."

"Dirty Art, do you want a hot dog?"

"Arbo!"

"Dirty Art, do you want to play baseball?"

"Arbo!"

Sometimes it meant yes and sometimes it meant no. After a few weeks of "Arbo" this and "Arbo" that, I began to answer him in the same way. Some days we would just say "Arbo" to each other.

We had a two-man fraternity, complete with a secret greeting, which required us to shake each other's hands for a solid minute. We also had a secret dance, in which we rapidly shuffled our feet back and forth. During the dance, we'd chant, "Zidzoo, Cramboo, Snerds." I claim to have made that up (as you'll see, I made up a lot of things).

One day, Dirty Art took me to Sandra Smith's house, on Belmont Street, near the Worcester State Mental Hospital (not that there was anything mentally off about her). Sandra went to a different junior high. She was a cute, slim girl, with freckles and shaggy brown hair. Joining us out on her house's white, wooden porch, she said, "I can't invite you in." She pointed to her father through the living room window, sitting there reading the *Worcester Telegram's* sports page. We hadn't been there long when Art positioned her up against the shingled wall. Yanking down her white underpants, he began to finger her. The rain drizzled as they went at it. I couldn't take my eyes off her dad.

Art and Sandra seemed to have done this before. At first, I was merely a student observer. Then Dirty Art insisted I try it. This never happened with Linda, not yet. I was afraid but, finally, I gave in. My middle finger went in like a vicar entering a church and came out like the bird on a cuckoo clock. Mind you, Sandra was very compliant. She seemed okay with the arrangement. She didn't even have to give me or Art a hand job. In the coming weeks, I went over to Sandra's without Art and fingered her on my own. She was always glad to see me. Of course, I didn't tell Linda.

Arthur and I hung out nearly every day after school. We went into the woods and smoked butts we found in gutters or ashtrays. Occasionally we were able to get our hands on a real pack of Camels or Luckies. He liked me because I made up original jokes—kind of profound one-liners. Someone told me that prisoners made up jokes—that prison was where jokes came from because they had nothing else to do. I didn't want to imitate those guys. I wanted to be creative, known for being *witty*—a good *Word Wealth* find. *Word Wealth* often gave me a sharp word when I needed it. But, I pissed off a lot of people. They called me a "wise guy." When you're a clever kid, you find out that dumb guys, most girls, and people in general, don't understand humor. They think you're making fun of them, and then, sometimes ... *wham!*

CHAPTER 3:

It's Hard to Make Friends

Over time, my life at Chandler changed for the worse. I was still in search of my identity, letting other kids influence me in a way that was not healthy. The school wasn't like May Street. It was more like a body of water—a weird lagoon—that had lots of tributaries. Kids flowed in from neighborhoods I'd never heard of. Like most junior highs, it thatched together different cultures, religions, and races in classrooms, gyms, auditoriums, and school-yards, where students could work out their differences—which sometimes meant beating the shit out of one another.

Roland Picard was a kid who punched out a lot of other guys during my three years at Chandler. Roland rolled up to school on a black Triumph, wearing a white T-shirt, a studded, black leather jacket, and black leather pants. He wore his greasy black hair in a pompadour, slicked back behind his ears in a duck's ass. He was clearly summoning Marlon Brando in *The Wild One*. Roland wanted to *be* Johnny Strabler. He must have been kept back a few grades, because he was older than every other student. If you stared at him, you would immediately get, "What the fuck are you looking at, asshole?" Everyone answered, "Nothin'."

Everyone was curious about him. Scumbags provoke curiosity and public interest. Roland had this girlfriend, Kay Perry, who was hotter than hell. Kay was about five-foot-eight, wore tight Levi's, and had big tits. She looked like a real fifties movie star—like Johnny Strabler's girlfriend, Kathie. She was from a rich family who lived on Salisbury Street and seemed excited to be going out with a boy from the wrong side of the tracks. During recess, Roland would take her into the nearby woods. She'd come back to class looking disheveled but satisfied.

Kay was way better-looking than Linda, but I wasn't about to mess around with her. It was hard enough for me to get Linda on the phone. I dialed her ten times for every time she picked up. We were still at different schools, so there was no way to run into her. And I still wasn't getting invitations to her family's golf club.

Meanwhile, I was spending more time with Dirty Art. He was friendly with rich kids I didn't know. Many of them lived on Salisbury Street. It was a line of demarcation in Worcester. If you mentioned Salisbury Street, that meant money. I called it "Power Drive" because residents of Salisbury Street had clout. And I wanted some of that. After all, the banks all had signs that told customers to "Think Big." In Worcester, some customers took that to mean they should rob the bank.

Some of the well-born Salisbury brats went to Chandler, but I knew they didn't want to be friends with me. That is, until one Saturday night in 1955, when I was thirteen. I called Dirty Art. He always answered the phone, "Yell-o." He asked me if I wanted to go to a party at Steve Burwick's house.

Steve's father, Charlie Burwick, was a partner in the law firm of Burwick and Burwick. Charlie was a large man and a big shot in Worcester. He was respected. I associated the word *respect*—as defined in my *Word Wealth*—with lawyers. Charlie was my father's lawyer. My father didn't really have much legal business to speak of—only when he needed a license to sell meat or vegetables. But Charlie was always happy to take my dad's

34

call. I recall his name and Pleasant number scribbled on the grocery store wall next to the pay phone—in pencil, in my father's nice-looking script. If Charlie Burwick called the store, all hell broke loose—like the Pontiff was calling. Stanley Smith, head stock boy and head of mispronunciation, would scream to my dad, "Hurry up! Mister Charlie Birdwick is on the phone."

Charlie made a lot of money as a personal injury lawyer. The 1950s marked the dawn of the whiplash era. Everyone in Worcester had whiplash, at one time or another, usually because someone rear-ended their vehicle. The body shop business boomed. So did Charlie Burwick's income.

Anyway, the party was at the Burwicks' handsome, split-level house. Steve's parents were away, in Cape Cod or New York City, so it was likely there would be girls, lots of them. The Burwicks belonged to the Mount Pleasant Country Club, like Linda's family. But I knew Linda wasn't part of Steve's clique. She'd told me she had only one friend: Bitty Baron, a tall and beautiful dirty blond, who lived practically next-door to Linda. Bitty's father was a doctor and was as strict as Linda's mom. So, it was a safe bet Bitty and Linda wouldn't be at the Burwicks.

The party would be the first time I'd ever been inside a house on Salisbury Street. Dirty Art's mom, Neddie Freedman, drove us there. Little Neddie could barely see over the steering wheel. She was so tiny it seemed she could fit into the car's ashtray.

When we arrived, Steve opened the imposing front door. His puffy smile and soft handshake went together. I will never forget his voice. It was tranquil and yet, every so often, he made a little squeak. I wondered if there was a chipmunk in his pocket. Steve was very friendly. I was beginning to feel at home. He introduced me to his girlfriend, Diane Itkin. Her father was a doctor. Lots of doctors in Worcester had beautiful daughters. I thought maybe they gave their daughters some medical treatment to make them beautiful. Bearing out my theory, Diane was a gorgeous brunette with large breasts. They jutted out like a serving tray under her neatly pressed, ruffled white shirt. Her breathy, Marilyn Monroe voice gave me goose bumps. But she was Steve's girlfriend, and I was going to honor that.

Diane confirmed to me that girls were everything. For the rest of my life, I couldn't give a shit about anything other than girls, beautiful girls, chasing them. I vowed that, whenever I got one, I would stare long and hard at her beauty.

The party started in the living room, which had a big fireplace. Steve put some 45s on an RCA portable record player that came in a small plaid suitcase that matched the girls' skirts. Steve had a good collection—some genuine rock and roll, like Big Joe Turner's "Shake, Rattle and Roll," as well as some dreamy stuff girls liked, like "Mr. Sandman" by The Chordettes. I never heard those songs at home because my parents listened to Broadway musicals like *Annie Get Your Gun* and sad operas like *Carmen*. Believe me, I suffered every time Carmen died on that record—while my mother sang the finale in our kitchen to the dirty dishes.

Everyone at the party started dancing, or "bopping," except for me, because, again, I was self-conscious. I thought only assholes danced because you looked like an asshole when you danced. So, I started telling Dirty Art a joke. I told one of mine and, before I knew it, I was standing on the hearth of that big fireplace telling jokes to the entire room—rapid fire, one after the other, all originals.

That's what some people do when they are feeling self-conscious. They stutter, then out comes a joke. It breaks up the place and everyone becomes less nervous. Kind of like a keyboard and what musicians do—play the scales up and then down until out comes a song. Until then, I used to tell myself made-up jokes and go hysterical. But I was probably crying inside. Now I was doing stand-up in Burwick's living room and getting laughs from all the cute girls in long wool pleated skirts. The guys, most of whom I didn't know, were laughing, too—pointing at me and asking, "Who is this very fucking funny guy?" My funny side always competed with my cool side.

In the fifties, girls really liked "sharp" guys. I thought sharp guys were not supposed to be funny. Funny also had a high standard. If you were trying to be funny, you had to be as funny as those Jewish comedians on television. Otherwise, no one would laugh.

I also had my own language, words I made up, expressions that no one ever heard before. I was calling guys "mon" before any Jamaican knew what the hell a "mon" was. "Ya, mon." So, I discovered that it wasn't difficult to maintain my cool exterior and be funny at the same time. Girls never seemed to notice me much before I turned thirteen. But all that changed at Burwick's party. Some girls started to tell me I looked like Paul Newman and I believed it. "Self-persuasion is no persuasion," my mother used to say.

On the way home, Dirty Art laughed in his pernicious way. He would get credit for bringing me to the party.

"Rich, you were great tonight!" he said. "I'm proud to be your pal. I thought you were going to embarrass me at first. But, fuck, you are a goddamned good joke teller. One funny son of a bitch. Where the hell did you learn to do that?"

"Yah, I had to become a professional comedian to make friends. I practice at home. My mother's hilarious when she's in the mood—cracking jokes when she's not cracking up."

"Your mother?"

"No, your mother!"

"No, your mother!"

"No, your mother!"

That was the way things went a lot of time between me and Dirty Art. We constantly insulted each other by saying your mother this or your mother that.

"Your mother works in the Navy Yard!"

"Your mother eats shit!"

"Your mother fucks your uncle!"

"Your mother is a whore!"

"Your mother sucks dick!"

Around this time the expression "suck" was hatched and everyone and everything sucked. It meant that there was a blow job involved, and people's jobs were directly connected to blow jobs because their job sucked. That meant, if you had such a job, the job gave you and other people a blow job. If a certain college sucked that meant that the entire faculty and the student body were available for blow jobs. If someone sucked, they would instantly give you a blow job. By the time I finished my childhood, everything and everybody sucked, and I believed that there was a pair of lips in the sky, as large as the Big Dipper, just waiting to suck you off and make you come or, as we sometimes said, make you "come off."

The day following the party at Steve's, the phone started ringing off the wall. We had a party line, PLeasant 47504—though we lived nowhere near anything pleasant. (When we lived in the tenement over my father's grocery store, we didn't use a phone; we'd just yell out the window.)

First, Steve called. He told me how funny I was and asked if we could play tennis together at Newton Square Park.

"Yes, I would love to play tennis," I replied.

"We play on Saturdays," he said. "I will meet you at one o'clock at Newton Square."

"Great, I really want to play you," I answered, not mentioning that I didn't have tennis balls or a tennis racquet or tennis clothes, or that I'd never seen a tennis match.

But I now had a second friend besides Dirty Art!

The phone rang again. It was Robert Kirsch. He was about 6'5", had a potbelly and spoke through his nose while twisting his large lips.

"Golub, you were pretty amazing last night," he said. "I would like to be your friend. Wanna come to my house and play poker with me and my father?"

"Sure, I would love to do that," I said, asking nervously, "Where do you live? Do I have to come over now?" (Obviously I was new at this.)

"4 Sherwood Road," he said. "Come around the back door. We'll be down in the basement." He added with a laugh: "Bring money!"

Wow, I now had *three* friends! I hadn't realized that being friends meant you had to bring money. Playing poker with Kirsch and his fat father, Irving, was weird but I guessed that is what being friends is like. I didn't have any money and I had never played cards, much less a game of poker. But if you want friends, you must endure. And I was determined to make good and lasting friends.

The next call was from Ronnie Meenes. Ronnie was sixteen and had just gotten his driver's license. He was fat and always had a king-size cigarette hanging from his lower lip.

"Hey, you're a funny guy," he said. "We're going to be friends. Why don't you come along with me when I sell ice cream tomorrow after school?"

His voice was gruff but sincere, and I could tell he really wanted to be my friend.

"Ice cream, sure," I enthused, "But how do you sell it?"

"You just jump into my ice cream truck. You don't need a white uniform. Just ride shotgun. We go around the neighborhood near Chandler. I ring the bell. Kids come running out of their houses with change. It's that simple. Kids are like birds in a bush. They pop out, get the ice cream, and we get their money."

This, too, seemed a bit crazy. Suddenly, I had to ride around in a truck and sell ice cream. But, hell, to make a *fourth* friend, I would do it!

"Do I get to eat any of the ice cream?" I asked. "A Popsicle maybe?" (Like any other kid, I loved ice cream and didn't get much of it, even though my dad owned a grocery store.)

"After we finish, if I make over twenty bucks, I will give you an ice cream sandwich. Deal?"

"Deal," I agreed, not knowing what a "buck" was. "You sound like a real friend."

Just as I hung up, the phone rang again.

"Hello, Richard? This is Barry Solomon. My friends call me Monk, and I'm also known as Manfred Krinx to certain good-looking women. We met last night. You are a very funny boy. So am I. We should be friends. I live on Salisbury Street. We have a pool table in the basement. Would you like to come over and play pool?"

"Pool? I never swam in a basement pool! That sounds like great fun!"

"Sorry, pool is a game that you play on a table with balls. You hit them with a stick and then they go into a hole."

"That is something I can do—hit a ball with a stick, like baseball. I would love to come over."

"And," Monk added, "then we can be friends. I also have a younger sister, named Debby, and she'd like to meet you."

He hung up. A *fifth* friend! "Man, I am really racking up the friends today," I said out loud. I was overcome by a warm feeling in my chest. Could this mean I was becoming popular?

The rest of the day I got more calls from other guys at the party. No girls called because that was the rule in the fifties. Girls never called guys, no matter how much they wanted to. Girls played the vicious game of "hard to get." Linda was a pro.

There was a lesson in these calls. My mother used to say that I didn't have a lot of brains, but I had "know-how." She didn't realize that what you say to children sticks for life. So, I put my "know-how" to work. If I didn't learn how to play the game—whether it was tennis, poker, pool, or selling ice cream, I wasn't going to have any friends. The basis of friendship was contributing something, usually a skill that your friend could exploit. The fact that I was a jokester meant I was qualified to engage in this symbiotic relationship. And, though we called each other friends, I might have to fight my friend or else wind up with the short end of the stick. I once heard someone say, "If you cannot sell your best friend your used car, who can you sell it to?" I heard someone in my father's grocery store take that logic a step further. "If you can't fuck your best friend's girlfriend or wife," the man said, "who can you fuck?" I would come to find out that the push and pull of friendship was going to be a large part of life. Friendship was a complex matter.

The guys who called me were all part of the same clique, though Steve Burwick didn't run with their pack. These guys did everything together: smoked, drank beer, played cards, played pool, you name it. If I wanted to be friends with them, I had to play their game or get the fuck out. There were seven of them. I was the eighth. So, we called ourselves the Crazy Eight, like the card game Crazy Eights. We were all avid card players. We never played a game as lame as Crazy Eights, but the name was fitting. It comes from the United States Army code, commonly known as Section 8, which governs the discharge of soldiers deemed to be mentally unstable.

Every day the Crazy Eight would meet at four o'clock. Ronnie Meenes would pick us up in his 1955 white Ford Victoria convertible—his ticket into the Crazy Eight—and drive us to Robbie Kirsch's place, where we'd open a new deck of Bicycle cards and play hours of poker. As time went on, the Crazy Eight became notorious—mostly among the mothers of eligible teenage Jewish girls—for being wild, out of control, and just plain trouble.

It's true that we intentionally bumped into girls in the corridors— apologizing as we copped cheap feels while our buddies laughed. We called this breast-investigation "bagging up" a girl. All the guys at Chandler were constantly trying to bag up girls, even though there wasn't much there to bag. After a while, when the girls saw you coming, they'd slap you before you tried.

Dirty Art was always introducing me to his collection of weirdos. They weren't off to the races like the kids in my neighborhood, but he had a knack for finding misfits. Their strangeness made them fascinating—draining and absorbing at the same time. "Wild Bill" Holloway, for instance. Moments after Art introduced me to him in the schoolyard, I could see Holloway's eyes blazed with madness. Perhaps it was a gene inherited from the first William Holloway, an early settler in Northboro, Massachusetts, who married a widow whose husband had been killed in an Indian massacre. That mix of terror and anger—like he'd just seen someone scalped, or maybe he'd just scalped someone—was on this Bill Holloway's face. He had a cratered pink complexion, worse than acne, more like chickenpox. He had yellow teeth and his head was practically square. Yet Dirty Art had befriended him.

"What are you doing tomorrow after school?" asked Holloway, his dirty T-shirt soaked with sweat.

"I haven't thought about it," I said. "Maybe play basketball. Do my homework."

"Dirty Art and I are going someplace," Holloway said mysteriously. "You wanna come?"

Dirty Art said, "Arbo!"

Art was up for it, but I sensed that nothing good could come from going anywhere with Holloway.

I threw my green book bag over my shoulder and was about to walk home. I thought this conversation had ended. But suddenly, Holloway jumped in front of me, blocking the way.

"Richie, I said we have plans tomorrow," he stressed. "Are you coming along?"

Questions occurred to me: Were these kids going to rob a bank? Rape a girl? Shoplift? Who the hell knew?

"I don't know," I hedged. "My mother's waiting for me down the street." That was a lie, but Holloway let me pass.

The next day, at school, Dirty Art looked different. His smug expression was gone. He appeared nervous. When classes got out, I caught up with him in the school driveway on May Street. He and Holloway were sitting in a two-door, red-and-black 1956 Mercury. Holloway was in the driver's seat, smoking a cigarette butt. Gray gas fumes oozed out of the Merc's dual exhaust. Holloway kept revving the engine as if it were a musical instrument.

"Get in!" Dirty Art yelled to me from the passenger side. "Get the hell in! Arbo! Arbo!"

I knew right away what was going on. I'd seen stolen vehicles parked in my old neighborhood. The thieves were father's customers.

"That car is stolen," I said. "No way! I am not getting in!"

Holloway looked like a vampire eager to take strike.

"Fuck you, Golub, just fuck you!" Holloway shouted. "This is my old man's car! So, fuck you!"

"Your old man lets you drive without a license?" I asked, scared shitless.

"I said get in!" Dirty Art ordered.

Just then, his head snapped back as Holloway put the pedal to the metal. The thick-treaded white sidewall tires screeched as the Mercury "scrubbed out," roaring toward the gym, headed at three faculty members Holloway hated: the gym teacher, Mr. Bennett; Mr. Ryan, the assistant principal; and Mrs. Ryan, his wife, our English teacher. The three were chatting near the school's back entrance. They jumped out of the way of Holloway's corpse-maker. Holloway slammed on the brakes, turned the Mercury on two wheels, and nearly ran over some schoolyard kids who ran for their lives.

There was no setting the clock back on this one. Dirty Art had turned a corner in life that would identify him for years to come. Shit, bank robbers stole cars for getaways; ordinary kids didn't swipe automobiles. Mostly, they just shoplifted at the five-and-dime.

Later that day, the Worcester Police arrested Dirty Art and Holloway. The front page of the *Worcester Telegram* bellowed, "2 YOUTHS JAILED." The perpetrators' names were not reported as they were "juveniles" (a word I thought referred to Jewish kids who lived on the Nile river). But everyone knew it was Dirty Art and Holloway. Worcester was scandalized, Art and Holloway were just a couple of schmucks in a Mercury. But some people compared them to Sacco and Vanzetti, the anarchists accused of murdering two men in a robbery in 1920. (Judge Webster Thayer, who controversially sentenced the Italian immigrants to death, lived in Worcester in a house that was later blown up by vigilantes. Every year, two unidentified men would piss on his grave in Hope Cemetery.)

I never asked Dirty Art how many times he said "Arbo" to the cops. His dad, Joe Freedman, was ready to beat the hell out of him. Art's arrest put me in a better light. It was far worse than urinating on Miss Michelle. Art had made the front page. Some people spoke of Holloway and Freedman as if they were already legends. Their ill-considered act of adolescent rebellion awakened memories of two revolutionaries whose conviction stirred protests around the world. It was ridiculous, but that's the way Worcester talked. I was glad the cops caught them quickly. With Holloway at the wheel, I had the wild thought, the two might have gone on a rampage, as teenage spree killer Charlie Starkweather did a few years later. You never know.

The last time I saw Holloway he told me to "Suck a hardshe!" That expression was a Worcester version of suck that never was defined or understood.

This was the fifties.

CHAPTER 4:

Public School Wasn't for Me

In 1957, when I was close to graduating from Chandler and after I'd begged my parents until they couldn't stand it anymore, they let me apply to Worcester Academy. Founded in 1834, it sat atop Union Hill, looking down upon the gritty city. Its campus—a word I loved as much as the name Linda Paul—rambled across thirty acres. Ivy climbed the red brick buildings. The students lived in dorms and wore repp ties, weejuns, and seersucker. Cole Porter, a Siamese prince and various captains of industry had attended. Its Lewis J. Warner Memorial was a contribution from the movie studio. But, most significantly, Linda's brother, Richie Paul, went there. I wanted to prove that I was his equal, if not his better.

Worcester Academy was another private world I was trying to quarry my way into—a fortified realm like Andover, Phillips Exeter, St. Paul's, Taft, Deerfield, Groton, and other boarding schools whose very names were so intimidating that just pronouncing them made your teeth feel insignificant. I knew my parents didn't have the bucks to send me off to one of those places. But I still imagined downing a Budweiser with some lad named Chip or Kip and casually saying "prep" repeatedly.

Even so, I knew I was kidding myself because I was a natural-born maverick. That's right, it was in my blood to rebel. But my rebellion was always well thought out, and ultimately limited, like the guy who wraps his fist in a handkerchief before he punches out a windowpane. I was starting to feel like it might be time to stop rebelling against the world's assholes and start complying with the gatekeepers.

Despite my checkered school record and sketchy Certificate of Attendance, I was miraculously accepted. I cannot recall how my parents came up with the money to pay the tuition. Living in a dorm like Dexter Hall was too expensive, so I would be a "day hop," living at home.

I was admitted on the condition that I brush up on my math and reading at the Academy's summer school. Abbie Hoffman was taking a course or two there that summer. We bonded because of my friendship with his brother Jack. The Hoffmans lived around the corner at 6 Ruth Street, in a white bungalow, five minutes from us. (Their housekeeper, Flo, gave Jack and Abbie's friends blow jobs on a moment's notice.) I had memory problems. Abbie insisted on teaching me how to hypnotize myself so I could memorize all the course material. I spent hours with him waving a gold chain in front of my face. For two months, I tried to put myself into deep trances that would infuse my brain with trigonometric functions. It sounded nuts but it worked for Abbie; he got straight A's.

My remedial reading course was taught by John Metcalf, a seventy-year-old Mainer who had the jowls of a basset hound. He'd stretch his floppy dewlap to bay words that were barely recognizable. He wore the same threadbare houndstooth jacket every day and peered at you menacingly through thin metal spectacles. He specialized in poor readers. I was a great reader, and I didn't know what I was doing in this class of four. Metcalf was known as "Metty the Jaw." He'd been a major league pitcher and had gotten his jaw broken by a line drive.

Despite his age, Metty still had an arm. One beautiful July afternoon, he called on the kid behind me to read aloud. The sun shining on his curly head of hair, the kid came to the sentence: "The police roped off the area." Very slowly, he read: "The police raped off the area." Metty went nuclear. He fulminated at the poor kid. Then he picked up a hardcover copy of Webster's dictionary, wound up, hurled it at the kid, throwing a perfect strike. The dictionary hit the student smack in the forehead, knocking him off his chair. Damn, that must have really hurt.

"That's what you get for being stupid!" Metty barked. The kid put his head down on the desk and wept.

Around this time, I started exploring routes out of Worcester. I'd been riveted by Sen. Joseph McCarthy's televised witch hunt for Communists—especially his clash with the Army's lawyer, Joseph N. Welch. What really caught my eye were the congressional pages, the boys who delivered vital messages. I knew those little bastards must be having a ball running through the marble halls of Congress, rubbing shoulders with reporters, eavesdropping on closed-door sessions. Pages went to school at the Library of Congress. Plus, they got to wear a cool uniform with knickers. It was a prestigious position. I had it all figured out—I'd live in D.C. with my mother's political gadfly brother, Reuben Plevinsky, and his short, round wife, Clara. I asked my father's longtime customer, Rep. Harold Donohue, if he'd sponsor me for a pageship. He did my dad the favor of submitting my application, but I didn't become a page. I was very disappointed.

I pressed on with my after-school job, working as a stock boy in my father's grocery. His grandfather, Aaron Golub, had started the Green Street Market, one block from the famous Table Talk Pies, whose plant infused the air with the smell of flakey bakery goods. (Lemon meringue pie competed for your nose's attention with the odor of rancid beer coming from Green Street's saloons.) My grandfather sold penny candy in a shop that was then the size of a closet. He died before I was born. My father never told me much about him, just that Aaron Golub emigrated from Russia to South Africa, where the government granted him the first license to collect scrap metal from the battlefields of the Second Boer War. My grandfather picked up an unspent shell one day and it blew up in his face. The explosion left him blind in one eye and nearly blind in the other. He needed his two sons to help him in the store almost from the time they could walk.

My Uncle Izzie was born in 1912, my father in 1914. When my grandfather died in the 1930s, they took over. My dad usually worked the cash register and the meat counter. Izzie oversaw fruits and vegetables. They looked up to each other. Izzie once said, "Cut him and I bleed."

* * *

As I sweated through my summer classes and my summer job, Linda frolicked at Camp Kear-Sarge in New Hampshire—one of those rich kid getaways, with Indian names, run by residents of New York City's West Side. We wrote to each other every few weeks. My handwriting was craggy, appearing as if I had a grudge against expression. Hers flowed like little clouds on a summer day. I scratched out anguished confessions of longing. She shared nonsense about what happened at general swim. She also let me know that lots of kids from New York City were there. Her constant chatter about New York City alienated me. I knew the day was coming soon when she would go down the road to Manhattan and acquire a whole new set of friends. I knew I would come down for the weekend on a Greyhound bus, find out about her big time Wall Street boyfriend, then return to Worcester to sit at our kitchen table, pouring my heart out to my mother. It was as clear to me as an olive in a martini.

But New York City worked in my favor one weekend after Linda returned from camp. It was a Saturday when she called to inform me that her parents had departed for NYC and that she was home alone.

I raced to 15 Kensington before you could say English breakfast tea.

We immediately went up to her bedroom. It was decorated all in pink and seemed like it was made from velvet. We promptly took our clothes off and hopped into her warm bed. At first, we just lay next to one another, as if we were waiting for the bus. Gradually, we started to kiss. I touched her breasts, then went down below. The room began to sway. We turned into feral creatures, pawing our way through a primeval forest we never wanted to leave. I had the stiffest hard-on of my life. That Saturday, in 1957, I put that hard-on inside Linda Paul. I moved it in and out, imitating what I'd once seen Dirty Art do with Sandra in the woods. Like Sandra, Linda seemed to be enjoying herself. I could tell she was excited. I know it was the apex of my sex life, certainly up till then. Around 5 p.m., when it was getting dark, we were still lying silently next to each other when she said something weird.

"I am still a virgin," she announced.

Not being an expert on these matters, I replied, "Strange, I thought that I was inside, far inside."

"But you didn't break my hymen," she stated with absolute medical certainty.

"That's something I wouldn't know about," I confessed.

"Hymen" sounded like the first name of one of the panhandling rabbis who'd ask my father to donate to Israel. In the Old Testament it is written, in Samuel, that man can see only the outside of other humans and only God can see the inside. But I felt I now "knew" Linda, in the biblical sense. I had insight into her pussy.

I had screwed only one other girl in my life. Anita G. had been my babysitter when my family went to the beach in Onset, Massachusetts. I was thirteen. She was sixteen, tall, and attractive. She picked me up after I'd been playing pinball and showed me how to use my fingers for something other than manipulating flippers to bang steel pinballs around. She led me to a sandy cove near the two-lane concrete bridge that connects Onset to

Buzzards Bay. She unfolded a beach towel, slipped a Trojan onto my hard dick, and laid me. To show my appreciation, I took her to Kenny's Salt Water Taffy afterward for some peanut butter fudge.

As I left Linda's house and walked down Kensington Road, I asked myself whether what we'd just done was all a dream. It wasn't, but, during our next five years of dating, Linda continued to claim she was a virgin. I banged her in cars, on couches, sometimes even in beds. But she insisted her hymen was intact. In the fifties, guilty virgins were as common as Wurlitzer jukeboxes.

Linda's body wasn't that hot. She was flat-chested and had small shoulders. But her skin was soft, and her ass was curvaceous. Her biggest assets were her long legs. She was a refined beauty, more like Audrey Hepburn than Bettie Page. In my clearest memory of her, she's wearing a short, black, wool skirt, dark pantyhose, flat shoes, and a white, round-collar blouse that buttoned down the front. It was a look I couldn't resist: an insatiable Sybarite disguised as a prim librarian.

Of course, now that Linda was back, her family did its best to keep me away from her. Now that fall classes were starting at Worcester Academy, I had to run into Linda's imperious brother all the time. Richie Paul was a class ahead of me. Not only was the six-foot-four prick the captain of the basketball team, but he was also captain of the swimming team, always strutting around bare-chested in his Speedo. Meanwhile, I could barely float.

Maybe I was trying to impress Linda—and her jock-star bro— when I decided to try out for the football team. Since I knew a lot about pro sports, I convinced myself that I was a running back. I had played football at Chandler, but was never a star. At the time, I was only about five-foot-six. Linda was slightly taller than me. Worcester Academy had some good players. Like many prep schools, it allowed promising high school athletes to do a postgrad year to improve their academic records and show their stuff to college scouts. Numerous WA grads had gone on to the NFL— the 49ers, the Packers, the Colts, you name the team. Against everyone's advice, I tried out as a halfback. Practice took place at Gaskill Field (emphasis on the "kill"). My first few scrimmages went well. I was fast in my cleats. I loved the huddles—a bunch of guys planning something cool. The quarterback, Augustus "Gus" Wagner III, would say "hut," a word the Roman centurions used to make the troops march in time. I was standing proudly in the backfield one day when Gus grunted "hut" and handed me the ball. I saw a hole, between the right tackle and the center, and ran toward daylight, thinking, "Shit, this is easy. I'm going for a touchdown!" From out of nowhere, John Swinnerton hit me so goddamned hard that I blacked out. I woke up on the ground, staring at the 4 p.m. sun, surrounded by my teammates. My left leg was in excruciating pain.

"My leg," I said. "It's broken! I know it's broken!"

Gus ordered everyone to stand back. "I got this one," he said. "Let's call an ambulance."

He and the other players pointed to my right leg, mumbling that it looked busted. They helped me stand on my "good leg," plunging me into deeper pain. I bit my lip, too embarrassed to tell them they had the wrong leg.

I knew I would never wear a red-and-white cardigan letter sweater. But hobbling around campus with my sports injury was kind of cool. My cast was a great attention-getter.

CHAPTER 5:

Bad Influences

The teachers at Worcester Academy shoveled on tons of difficult homework. We got out of classes in the late afternoon. There wasn't much time for goofing around with the Solitro Brothers or Stanley Toomey, or playing raisin bread poker with the patients at Fairlawn. Dirty Art's parents reined him in after his arrest, but he and I still got together with the Crazy Eight. We were a tightly woven group. We moved like a hand-knit sweater, each of us a loop. We still played seven-card stud or poker at Bo's house, with Bo and, clad in his boxer shorts, his father, Irving, who, by the way, was the foreman at Linda's dad's hat factory. No one ever won, except Irving, who would deal. I always thought Bo was in cahoots with Irving until one day when Irving ordered Bo to cut the deck. Bo replied, "Dad, cut this!" Whereupon Bo lifted his leg and unleashed a ripsnorter for the ages. The games always left me flat broke. After the first couple of hands, I had to scrounge money from the other guys so I could continue to lose.

I already mentioned five of the Eight. There was also Ed Dworkin. We called him "Muffin" because he was a well-known "muff diver." Muffin was his rightful and well-deserved "cardinal" name. Cardinal names were our version of cardinal rules. They were fundamental. Rick Seder's cardinal name was "Rick the Prick," because of his wicked sarcasm—probably extracted from his brilliant mother, Ruth, who had her personal copy of *Word Wealth.* (She and I used to dissect words in the Seders' breakfast nook.) Rick once caught trustworthy Dirty Art screwing Sue Abelsky, Rick's girlfriend, in her basement. They patched it up—Rick and Art, that is; I'm not sure about Rick and Sue. Joel Robbins was a sharp guy with curly black hair. He was an ace tennis player. His cardinal name was "Leoj Snibbor"— Joel Robbins spelled backward.

Ronnie Meenes was "Meenie Peenie Tinkle." Bob Kirsch was "Slobby Robby." We stuck to those names as if we were born with them. I don't think anyone else in Worcester knew those names or was allowed to use them. Not that anyone was clamoring to use them.

No one else in the Crazy Eight went to Worcester Academy, or wanted to. They were quite happy in their public high schools—particularly after I told them how hard WA's classes were. Believe me, I tried to study. But it was damn difficult to concentrate. I have a nomadic mind. Muhammad Ali's musician father, Cassius Clay, Sr., suffered from a speech defect that stemmed from his trying to say everything he thought at once. I could relate. The world's biggest playground was in my head. I'd be trying to solve a geometry problem when my mind would be invaded by Mickey Mantle's batting average, or my possible future as a film star, or Linda taking off her bra.

Because I wasn't so great academically, I had to stay late in study hall, located in an underground auditorium. One night I couldn't concentrate, so I pulled out J.D. Salinger's *The Catcher in the Rye*, published a few years earlier. I was obsessed by its hero, Holden Caulfield, an alienated, girl-crazy sixteen-year-old, who gets kicked out of Pencey Prep. Something about his story rang true. After reading a few pages, I turned around and saw about fifteen other guys also reading *The Catcher in the Rye*. Maybe we were all racing to find out how our own stories would end.

For me and some other guys, it wasn't a matter of *if* we'd get in trouble; at Worcester Academy, it was when. Just before I started at WA, I struck up a friendship with another student, Jack Moosa. His father was Worcester District Court Judge Walter J. Moosa. Jack looked like Lou Ferrigno, the bodybuilder. He was a big guy with a big head who drove a Turtle Waxed, fire engine red, '37 Ford roadster with a V-shaped front grill, dual exhausts, and a three-speed floor shift. He invited me to ride shotgun. I knew some of the spark plugs in Moosa's head were misfiring. But I couldn't resist getting into his souped-up car. Its huge engine could shoot it over 120 miles per hour. Mostly Moosa used his car for bird-hunting. He would crawl along a dirt road at five mph in first gear, creep up on a pigeon, then swiftly release the clutch, slam-shifting into second gear while flooring the accelerator. In the process, he would run over the pigeon.

His vocabulary devolved primarily on the well-worn Worcester expression word "suck." Moosa would drive down bustling Main Street, on a Wednesday night, when the stores were open until 9 and Worcester hummed with shopping excitement. He'd roll down his window and holler, "SUUUUUCK!!!!" His ungodly voice echoed in the downtown canyons, startling passersby who wondered who on earth had uttered this thundering obscenity.

One night, Moosa spotted me going into Ware Pratt, Worcester's oldest clothing store for boys, with my parents. He screamed, "Golub, you suck!" You cannot imagine the shock on my dad's face. By then, Moosa had vanished down a side street.

Richie Lariviere was another rich kid with a knockout car and a bad attitude probably because a tough kid named Ray Matarazzo supposedly punched him in the neck when he was very young, possibly causing Richie to grow a malignant tumor in his throat. Half of his neck was surgically removed. He also knew a lot of jokes and drove a green-and-white 1957 Chevy Impala convertible, with dual exhausts and a louvered hood. Worcester had a lot of garages that specialized in lowering a car's rear springs to give it a hot rod appearance. Body shop surgeons could "chop" a car (lower its roof), "channel" it (remove and raise the floor so the car sat close to the pavement), or both. Hot rodders decorated their rigs with flames and skulls, using fluorescent Day-Glo paint, previously available only to the military.

Everyone wanted a piece of "cool"—a word just coming into its own in the mid-fifties—and Richie Lariviere's Chevy was cool.

Lariviere could be a little fiendish but then, so could I. The two of us weren't exactly following the Academy's motto—"Achieve the Honorable"—one dreary day in January of 1958. That morning, we arrived early at school in his Chevy, parking it on Providence Street outside the wrought iron gates. Inside his trunk was a mother lode of fireworks he'd just purchased, in Florida, during Christmas break. Before most people were on campus, we slipped into the school's main building, Walker Hall, and planted an orchard's worth of cherry bombs, strung together with long red fuses.

Like angelic little boys, we proceeded to morning chapel, where all students were expected to sing off-key hymns like *Onward, Christian Soldiers*. (I mostly hummed. I'd worked too hard for my bar mitzvah to surrender now to the Word of Christ.) Following the first-class period, many students and teachers hit Walker Hall's basement rec room, known as "The Spa," where you could get ice cream sundaes, cigarettes, or even Cuban cigars.

During this recess, at 9:45 sharp, we lit the fuses from our assigned posts. Simultaneously, about a hundred cherry bombs exploded. It sounded like the D-Day invasion. It was absolute bedlam. The faculty freaked, but students ran excitedly through the corridors, as if it were the beginning of summer vacation.

It didn't take long before the faculty discovered the perpetrators of this Guy Fawkes Gunpowder Plot. I was the first to be hauled into the office of Dean Harold D. "Dutch" Rader. As usual, Dean Rader's fly was wide open. His hairy ears gave him a baboonish appearance. Rader taught algebra, or tried to. My friend Jack Hoffman, Abbie's brother, once told him he didn't understand algebra. "So what? I've been teaching it for twenty-five years and I don't, either." Without uttering a word, Rader shepherded me down the Persian carpeted hall to the office of Headmaster William S. Piper.

Piper was a stern, broad-shouldered man who had a full head of brown hair. He favored the classic Mr. Chips look—gray three-piece suits with a gold pocket watch tucked into his vest. He sat behind an oak desk. Like the desk, one of his legs was made of wood—the result of a World War II injury.

"You know why you are here," he stated. It wasn't in a question form, so I didn't answer.

"This type of behavior will not be tolerated," he went on, "not at Worcester Academy!"

Clearly the headmaster was trying to convey the gravity of my actions. But I couldn't help thinking of how, in the Navy, sailors call the toilet the "head." So, Piper was really the Toilet Master. I looked at his pocket watch and imagined him emerging from his mother's womb buttoning his three-piece suit. That's my knack for the ridiculous. I thought his lecture was much ado about nothing. They were just cherry bombs! I suspected that, on some level, even Piper thought we'd livened up the day. I bet his son, who was two years ahead of me at WA, got a kick out of the prank.

Piper prepared to issue his verdict.

"You are expelled!" he announced. As he issued his ultimatum, he nodded at Rader. For a moment, I thought he was expelling Rader. But, with a gleeful look, Rader informed me, "You are to leave the premises immediately."

I never understood why I had to leave right away. Why couldn't I leisurely return to The Spa, smoke a Lucky, and have a nice hot chocolate before braving the wilds of winter?

As I walked out of Piper's office, I looked up at his old secretary for a speck of maternal sympathy. It was usually easy for a sad-eyed boy to get. She glared over her wire-rimmed glasses as she dropped a balled-up piece of paper into her trash basket. It probably had my name on it.

I went to the cloakroom to fetch my coat. I saw Richie Lariviere climbing the steps to Piper's office. He didn't acknowledge me, and I felt sorry for his decimated neck. I was hoping he might take responsibility for the bombing. But maybe he was going to blame it on me. I saw him grinning like a barracuda. I didn't get it then, but he must have figured his parents would make a large gift to the school and Richie Lariviere would be back in class.

I never found out who'd squealed on us, but there was a rat somewhere in those ivy-covered buildings. Snitching was the worst thing a kid could do to another kid, but the school was full of snitches.

I looked out the window. A blizzard was raging. I couldn't make out the branches of the elm trees, or even the sky. I stepped outside. The snow was up to my knees. An hour ago, I was surrounded by kids, eating a Mars Bar, laughing myself silly, thinking we'd never be caught.

I would've taken the bus, but I'd spent all my money at The Spa. Walking down Providence Street, passing folks shoveling the sidewalk, I realized that I was freezing. I wasn't wearing a heavy coat. Large flakes covered my face and hair like a suffocating white plastic bag. My lips were turning blue. I was beginning to feel sorry for myself.

By now, I was an old hand at getting expelled. For all my bravado, it always ignited a horrible feeling in my chest. I might joke about getting the boot from a man with a wooden leg. But I felt degraded and ashamed.

I'd struggled to get into WA and now, after one semester, I was out. I felt like I was slipping below the surface of the earth.

Why was it that I continued to pull weird shit wherever I went? Maybe I was getting to be one of those misfits. I certainly didn't deserve to be a congressional page. My grammar school report card made it plain: "Richard does not work well with others."

As I trudged down the hill, my misery compounded. I passed my old nursery school, where, when I was three, I'd bitten another kid's arm. I'd drawn a little blood. The preschool teacher in the long brown skirt told me, "Get out and walk home!" It was a snowy day just like this one. How the hell could a so-called teacher tell a three-year-old to walk home alone? It was over a mile, too. But I gritted my baby teeth and started walking. When I got to Water Street, I saw a feeble old lady standing nervously on the curb. I took her hand and helped her cross the street. At three years old! How bad could I be?

Now I plowed ahead again. I took the longest possible route to my dad's store. I was avoiding the inevitable conversation with him. Although I am sure he would have made me feel better, I just couldn't. He'd struggled to pay my WA tuition. When we went shopping at Ware Pratt, I wanted to buy one of those tweedy brown sports coats with leather buttons, so I'd fit in at WA. Dad unhesitatingly said, "Go and charge it to my account." It was expensive—$14. My mother threw a fit, and railed for days, about the price. It took him a year to pay off his layaway plan. One of my cousins told me, long after my dad died, that he was the wildest kid in the family. I never would've known. My dad didn't swear, smoke, or ever insult anyone. He was an old-school gentleman. Maybe there was hope for me.

* * *

A few days after my expulsion, Dean Rader called my parents and grudgingly permitted me to return to Worcester Academy. They also let Richie

Lariviere back in. I'd see him driving around in his Chevy. He'd wave or give me the finger, depending on his mood. Getting the finger, or giving it, was as common as plain pizza. Worcester kids thought they created the middle finger gesture. They didn't have a clue that even the ancient Greeks flipped the bird to tell one another to fuck themselves.

Anyway, I figured I'd better keep my distance from Richie Lariviere. The administration was watching my every move. I tried my best to be a model student. But I faced a new nemesis, more daunting than any I'd met before: geometry.

The subject, without exaggeration, gave me a nervous breakdown. I had to master geometry to make it to the next grade. But I didn't understand a fucking thing about angles and planes. No sooner would I learn a theorem than I'd forget it. Night after night, I stayed up late studying. I started to get physically ill—throwing up. I had nightmares. In a typical one, a hose that stretched into infinity was stuck up my ass, loudly inflating me with air. I was getting larger and larger. I felt like vomiting, but I couldn't. I floated like a balloon over Worcester until a long silvery pin burst me into millions of geometric theorems. Then I would inflate over again.

It may sound funny now but at the time I thought I was cracking up. One night, my dad walked into my bedroom, stared at my disheveled bed and my disorganized desk and said, "Rich, what's happened to you? You used to be a happy-go-lucky kid."

"Geometry," I groaned.

The Academy recommended that my geometry teacher, John Quigley, who always dressed in shades of dark brown and lived in the faculty dorm, tutor me. He was a mousey, British man. He would invite me to his "rooms" for tutoring, always at night. My dad would wait patiently behind the wheel of his truck. He'd sit next to me, sharpening number two yellow pencils under a small brass desk lamp. I liked Quigley, but I didn't understand a word he said. I felt like a spy being grilled under a heat lamp. I wanted to cooperate, but my captor kept asking me questions I couldn't answer. Maybe it was Quigley's British accent, but I left there, on each occasion, more confused than when I entered.

I think I got a D in the class, but geometry had one benefit: It took my mind off Linda.

CHAPTER 6:

Into the Real World of Jobs

In the summer of 1958, I worked at Hammond Plastics, a factory owned by Carl Gordon, a sour-faced, white-haired, big-bellied man. Carl's three-story brick factory sat on a small pond that swallowed its chemical sewage. (Also near the pond was Maury's Deluxe Delicatessen. We used to joke that Maury fished his corned beef and pastrami out the pond, but that didn't stop us from eating Maury's "grinders" almost every day.) Hammond Plastics allowed Carl to build a nice wooden ranch house, on Salisbury Street, not far from the Burwicks. (Worcester was full of ranch houses, but I never saw any livestock.)

Carl had a short, muscular son, Mel, who drove a red Corvette. I don't know if you had to be an asshole to buy a Corvette, but Mel fit the bill. Probably owning a Corvette turned you into an asshole. I was less interested in Mel than Carl's daughter, Marilyn. She was a frosted brunette who could have been one of those "cheesecake" models I saw on a calendar hanging in a hot rod shop. She wore starched white shirts that accentuated her magnificent chest. I sometimes wondered how she fit inside her four-door Buick. Her breasts were very firm; I can vouch for that.

Every day my dad drove me to Hammond Plastics. The temperature in the factory was over 90 degrees. No wonder they call these places sweatshops. Working at Hammond came with more responsibility than I'd had at other summer jobs. At fifteen, I was running a machine that made plastics. You'd load powdered resin into an aluminum hopper at one end. The resin would be "extruded" through a long rectangular pan of scalding-hot water, coming out at the other end. I had to catch hot plastic pellets in a bag. It was a nonstop process—me vs. Extruder #9. I was John Henry, the steel-driver, or Lucille Ball in the chocolate factory. If I didn't keep up with Extruder #9, red hot, melting plastic would wind up all over the floor. When that happened, the foreman would shut down the machine and scream at me. He screamed at me at least ten times a day—until I was fired. I punched out for the last time before the end of June.

I mentioned my discharge to Bunny Pemstein, our ranch house neighbor who'd always liked my big words. Bunny also owned a plastics factory. There were a bunch of plastic factories in Worcester. Plastic was evidently the way to success. "Success" was the goal in the fifties. People talked about it nonstop. I am still talking about it. Thanks to plastic, the Pemsteins and the Gordons were all able to fly down to Florida in the winter and stay at the Fontainebleau, where they'd cha-cha-cha in the Boom Boom Room. Carl and Bunny played golf, with Linda's family, at the Mount Pleasant Country Club. I imagined them teeing off on Saturday while my dad, in his bloody butcher's apron, weighed hamburger meat to sell to welfare recipients.

Bunny asked me if I'd like to work in his plastics company. Bunny ran his operation out of a large ramshackle factory on the opposite side of town from Hammond Plastics. It didn't make anything; it was more like a plastics junkyard. Giant wheels with steel teeth, called garnets, chewed up scrap plastic and rolled it into bales. Sometimes I'd have to chop up the recycled plastic, which is how I got my Crazy Eight cardinal name—"Chopper the Man." Chopping could be risky. I once saw a woman lose four fingers.

They fell onto the floor, bloody and still twitching. It was a nasty place to work. Gathered on the loading bay were misfits who didn't like anyone, not even themselves.

My foreman went by the name "Big Joe." His worldview can only be described as testicular. From the get-go, he wanted to know if you had balls and if they were big. He only wanted workers with "big balls." If you were going to work for Big Joe, your balls—sometimes called "gonads" or "rocks"—had to be huge.

Big Joe's assistant was Beauregard Dupree, a thick-necked, 25-year-old lug with weatherbeaten skin. He lived in a peeling three-decker, with his mother, across the street from Bell Pond, another polluted body of water. It was just up the hill from the Worcester State Hospital, previously known as the Worcester Lunatic Asylum. Dating back to the 1830s, the hospital had frightening Victorian granite towers that made Fairlawn look like a nursery school. Patients roamed the grounds. Sometimes they wandered off into the city. I don't know if Dupree had spent time at Worcester State but, judging by his demeanor, he should have. When he walked, his head bobbed, and his shoes hit the floor heels first. A miasma of rotten eggs clung to him. One of my co-workers suspected it came from Dupree's nonstop farting. Often, Dupree would boast that he could outdo anyone at anything.

"I can out-swim, out-dance, out-run, or out-eat anyone," he'd say.

He hated me from Day One. He would follow me around muttering, "I am going to beat the shit out of you." Or he'd ask me, "Golub, did you ever take it in your head to make money?" If I said yes, he'd laugh, "Oh, you suck dick?!" Or he'd boast, "I fucked your mother." Living in Worcester, I'd gotten used to meeting people who claimed to have been intimate with my mom. If you got into a fight, or wanted to, sooner or later someone would need to say he'd fucked the other guy's mother. Or, to keep it fresh, someone might recall fucking the other guy's sister. Of course, one of you needed to have a sister.

One day when we were unloading a truck, Dupree made good on his threat, punching me in the back of the head in the loading station. I'd known this moment was coming. I turned and whacked him three times in the chin. He went down face-first. I wasn't a tough guy but something deep down inside me can explode. And Dupree was really getting to me.

Decking Dupree impressed Big Joe enough for him to admit, reluctantly, that I had big balls. But, considering that I'd assaulted his second-in-command, he was obliged to can me.

"Tell Bunny that I fired you," Big Joe yelled.

Bunny would sometimes call me into his glass-enclosed office to tell me a dirty joke or ask me if I was "getting any." That day, I found him sitting with his feet up on his regal, hand-carved wooden desk, smoking a long cigar and flirting with some woman on the phone. He was wearing a golf shirt with a little appliquéd golf ball, a plaid cardigan sweater, and his favorite black golf slacks. (Expensive pants were called "slacks" in the fifties.) Obviously, he was about to leave for a golf game, but he beckoned me with a crooked finger to sit down. Like so many other times when I'd sat in front of a lofty desk, I folded. I wasn't about to argue over this shitty job. He went mad on me. I tried to remember that Bunny was a family friend and that he really liked my parents (although I never saw him shop at my dad's store or ever talk to my dad for more than a few seconds). He was now acting very un-bunny-like. He forever gave me a bad impression of rabbits.

Working at Bunny's plastics plant, and at Carl Gordon's, taught me two important lessons: I didn't want to work by the hour or for anyone else. From that summer on, my greatest fear was that I would wind up working in a factory in Worcester for the rest of my life. What would Linda and her family think of that? Her father *owned* a goddamned factory. He didn't let his own children work there. Worcester was full of factories. I wondered if all of them were linked together like sausages. Was I supposed to work at one of them after another until I reached the final shit cartridge—The Hebrew Cemetery—then buried by a bearded rabbi?

Even though I'd gained essential insights into labor, I wasn't about to race home and tell my parents I'd lost my second summer job. I first needed to find a card game and lose some money. So, I walked up to Newton Square, which is not really a square but more of a roundabout that everyone in Worcester spins through at least once a day. When I arrived, around 5 p.m., an unusually large crowd was watching a five-card poker game going on behind the granite Second World War monument. The crowd included some of the Crazy Eight—Bob Kirsch and Ricky Seder. Playing in the game was Charlie Tapper, a thin, jumpy Jewish guy about two years older than us. Charlie spoke with a slushy lisp. He knew some good jokes, many of them original. He always wore white tennis clothes at Newton Square because playing tennis was considered cool.

Charlie was going head-to-head for big money—fifty bucks a hand— against Francis "Toastie" Santos, whose dad, "Jigger" Santos, was allegedly a Mafioso. Yes, Worcester had rackets—starting with gambling and booze and finishing with bookies. The legendary Rhode Island crime boss Raymond L.S. Patriarca was from Worcester—which, along with Providence and Boston, formed the unholy trinity of New England organized crime. Jigger Santos lived in the Tatnuck neighborhood. Word was that a perpetual basement card game went on at his house on Iowa Street—supposedly with a Tommy gun-toting guard stationed at the cellar door. Toastie Santos already had his own gang, the Tatnuck Square Boys.

Anyway, back to the Newton Square card game. Charlie was winning when, out of nowhere, Toastie accused him of cheating. Charlie did have a reputation for dealing off the bottom of the deck and palming cards. But nobody expected Toastie to take a swing at him. Charlie ducked and hit Toastie with a perfect shot to the jaw. Toastie's freckles seemed to jump off his face. I was in shock. No one ever thought Charlie was tough enough to stand up to Toastie, much less punch him in the jaw. In Worcester, the last thing you wanted was to get punched in the jaw because it meant the fight was going against you. Very soon you were likely to be unconscious.

Charlie pulled Toastie's yellow, wool, crew neck sweater over Toastie's head and pummeled him, eventually pinning Toastie to the ground with a headlock. (All fights in Worcester ended in headlocks.)

Toastie called out the three magic words: "I give up!"

Charlie loosened his grip and stood up.

Toastie, stunned, sheepishly walked to his car and drove up Pleasant Street toward Tatnuck.

That's my version of events. Steve Bean, a solid Worcester baseball player and one of Charlie's best friends, incorrectly remembers the trouble starting with Toastie walking around Newton Square looking for Jews to fight. Steve accepted the challenge, telling Toastie to take his pick: "Me or Charlie." Toastie chose Charlie because he was smaller. According to Steve, there was a long fight that reached a draw. Steve says he pulled Charlie away because he could see the tide turning in Toastie's favor.

In any case, we all knew the Toastie-Charlie fight wasn't the end of the story. Two hours later, at dusk, cars from Tatnuck—most of them two-door '53 Fords that had been disassembled and assembled many times just for fun—began to roll up to Newton Square. We were still there, standing like pathetic villagers awaiting the Visigoths. Out of those vehicles tumbled Toastie Santos, his brother Paulie, Johnny Aslanian, and Squeaky McGovern (no relation to Worcester's Squeaky Clean Car Wash), and the rest of the Tatnuck Square Boys. They moved on the balls of their feet, which was typical of tough kids in Worcester. (There were 10,000 Robert De Niros in Worcester.) They were coming for us tennis-playing Jews on our home turf.

The first kid they clocked was Lew Lebarsky, a big, goofy nerd, who'd just started a bodybuilding course. Lew wore tight T-shirts to show off his new muscles. He shadowboxed everyone he met, from the Good Humor man to the druggist at Izzie's Pharmacy. When he saw Squeaky McGovern walking across Highland Street with a lead pipe, Lew stood his ground—shadowboxing until Squeaky cracked the pipe on the back of Lew's crew-cut head. Squeaky had once told me he liked Jews, but his ecumenical spirit apparently vanished when a Jew burned Toastie. Lew lay on the pavement for a minute before brushing himself off and hobbling away.

Chaos ensued. Before I knew it, I was fighting two smaller Tatnuck guys and, weirdly, holding my own. I still don't know who those two guys were. All I recall is throwing and receiving punches nonstop.

Charlie was nowhere in sight. I heard the next day that his sweet mother drove her son and Steve Bean down to Cape Cod. They were going to stay down at the Cape until the whole mess blew over—like mobsters "going to the mattresses." There were other fistfights around the Square. Our morning-after analysis reckoned that the Jews had been beaten up badly and that the war would go on. There would be more punishment for what happened to Toastie. Charlie had fucked with the wrong guy and certainly the wrong family.

It had been coming for a long time. Worcester was rank with antisemitism. Jews accounted for about 25,000 of the total population of 182,000. The city was divided down the middle. Jews lived on the West Side and the East Side, but rarely on the North or South sides. I'd heard name-calling ("Dirty Jew," "Morta Christo"), but not until that night at Newton Square had there been outright tribal warfare. And it had broken out in the shadow of a memorial to those who'd fought the Nazis.

After that event there was an uncomfortable sense on the West Side. None of us went bumping along thinking Worcester was a nice place to live. Thick fear hung in the air that the Tatnuck Boys would return. The Revolutionary War had followed the Colonists' war with the Indians. Were the Jews the new Indians? Would we be wiped out next?

From time to time we received reassuring visits from liberal Democrats. Charismatic Sen. Jack Kennedy would drive down Main Street, revving up the Irish in Massachusetts' second-largest city. In 1956, when he was running for president a second time, Adlai Stevenson stuck his arm out his car window and shook my hand. He probably lost that election because he touched that misbehaving Golub kid.

* * *

Worcester Academy didn't invite me back. Leaving WA didn't break my heart. That fall, I enrolled in Classical High. It had a clock tower that looked like a minaret. Classical was one of Worcester's best public schools. But it was still torture to sit at a wooden desk watching a "teacher" fill a blackboard with information that would have been easier to speak, though that information still didn't have much use in my future. I'd had enough of school—period. I just didn't fit in. Or, as I preferred to see it, school didn't fit into my life. I certainly wasn't a real revolutionary, but I was revolting against teachers who had no understanding of students. Most of the kids had a bottomless tolerance for this process, especially the girls, who were my only diversion.

The one subject that interested me that year, when I turned sixteen, was Driver's Education. Like all kids, I was eager to get my license. I pictured Linda sitting next to me as I drove fast and smoked filter-tipped Marlboros. My father taught me the basic rules of the road—letting me take the wheel of his green, vegetable-scented '53 Chevy panel truck packed with boxes of grocery orders. After about a week of these lessons, I went for my official DMV road test along Quinsigamond Avenue. I had trouble getting the truck into first gear—the shift kept grinding and then I released it too fast. The Chevy leapfrogged down the avenue, causing the DMV examiner's head to hit the windshield.

"You flunked," he said, rubbing his forehead.

The second time I took the test, I drove our Dodge sedan and passed. The first night that I had my license, I begged my mother to let me take out the Dodge. After hours of arguing, she relented. I drove over to pick up Rick the Prick. Rick had been in a bad car accident the week before—the thick gauze around his head, his arm in a sling were clear evidence. Nevertheless, he was excited to join me on my first solo drive. We took a spin down to Salisbury Street. When we reached Flagg Street, I showed Rick how I could take a sharp corner with just my right pinkie on the wheel. I wanted to outdo Slobby Robby, whose pinkie could slip his 1955 Chrysler between any two double-parked cars.

We were cruising at 55 mph when I crashed into a curb. I jammed on the brakes. Rick's bandaged head slammed into the steel dashboard. The curb broke the Dodge's right front axle.

Rick was swearing at me as the tow truck hauled away the wobbling sedan. Naturally, the accident turned into a family crisis. My dad defended me, as usual. My mother decreed that, from then on, I had to be home by 11 p.m. She made sure I did, too. In rain or snow, she would stand at the bottom of our street—dressed in her white bedroom slippers and tattered wool nightgown—waiting for me to turn the corner. If I came home after 11, she would chase the Dodge up the street with a broom, banging on the roof and screaming, "You son of a bitch!"

All told, she must have called me a "son of a bitch" or a "bastard" or, oddly, a "bitch bastard" a million times. I would sometimes remind her that I was born legitimately at City Hospital, to a married couple named Golub, on September 18, 1942. Which she knew. Her bellicose chain of epithets was like a Tourette's outburst. I could have cooled her down if I'd given her even one curative hug. But that was a cold time—before people had discovered hugging.

* * *

For the first time in our lives, Linda and I went to the same school. But she kept me at a distance. We went out a few times a week, if you could call it going out. Her parents weren't traveling as much, so I didn't get to enter the pink room very often. We'd look for other spots to make out. We parked near Bancroft Tower, a turreted mini-castle built, in 1900, of boulders and cobblestones. It was the first place my dad took me when he returned from the war. Now I'd go there with Linda. On a good night, she'd let me unclip her bra and touch her nipples. Sometimes we'd be in her mother's car, which Linda called "Nandoom." When Linda was in a humorous mood, she'd say, "I am going to blow you in Nandoom." If she was going to blow me (and that was a rare treat), I had to wear a condom. Once I dreamt that her mother wanted me fitted for a full body condom.

After we turned fifteen, she constantly referred to her future life, as though she were a high society Edith Wharton character in *The House of Mirth*. And I, a grocer's son, was interrupting her ascent into New York society by just being the grocer's son, not a member of the right club. My last name rhymed with club but that was the closest I would ever get to the first green or the mahjong table. Our sexual attraction kept Linda and me together more than any mental connection. My most eruptive orgasms, in the front seat of my family Buick, were moments of truth backed by Linda wiping it off her lips, hands, and blouse. I didn't have to fantasize that I was anyone other than the grocer's son, whenever we pulled up to Bancroft Tower at midnight, knowing she was champing at the bit, next to me in the passenger's seat.

But, like most girls I knew, Linda dreamt about the day when some goddamn knight in shining armor would sweep her off her feet. She insisted on regularly going to Worcester's John W. Higgins Armory, the only museum in America devoted solely to arms and armor. The stain-glassed reliquary had thousands of medieval objects, including 24 complete suits of armor. None of them fit me. But among the lords of the Round Table (King Arthur's, not Dirty Art's), none could have been more chivalrous than I was as Linda's sixteenth birthday approached, in June 1959. Turning Sweet Sixteen was a big deal and, with only two years of high school left, I was determined to give her something that symbolized how deeply I loved her.

I had $250 saved in the bank and I was ready to blow it all on her. For weeks I agonized over what to get the girl who had everything. Finally, my mother asked, "Why don't you go down to Boston and see my Uncle Phil?"

"What's he going to do for me?" I replied.

"He can help you better than anyone," she said.

She had a point. Uncle Phil, her father's brother, a wan-faced antiques dealer, was known to have exquisite taste. He knew jewelry.

The following Saturday, I took a Greyhound bus to Brookline, where Phil lived in a white shingled bungalow. He answered the door in a rakish pair of plaid plus fours. He was a swank dresser and in amazing shape for his age. He was a strict vegan who swam every winter in the icy Atlantic. Women called him an Adonis. He was a "confirmed bachelor," dedicated to living life as he saw fit, not on a woman's terms. He was "that *Playboy* man," albeit with a Yiddish twist, before there was *Playboy*.

Uncle Phil instructed me to sit on his small, red velvet couch opposite his back while he listened, for over an hour, to the CBS weekly stock market quotations on a Bakelite radio. Finally, he turned around and clicked off the radio.

"Why do you want to give this Linda something so expensive?" he asked, truly baffled.

"Because the more expensive it is the better it will be," I replied. "Someone told me, 'You get what you pay for.'"

"No, that isn't true," he smiled. "There's one thing you have to look for, and it doesn't relate to how expensive it is."

"What's that?" I asked, but he didn't answer me.

"Richard, go into my hall closet," he pointed. "Try on the new topcoat."

This was another of Phil's rituals—showing me his latest sartorial acquisitions. He was proud not only of their fine tailoring, but of the bargain he'd gotten. Inside a large cedar closet, I found two racks of never-worn garments with sales tags that showed the mark-down from their original eye-popping prices. I unzipped a long navy-blue bag and found a handsome, brown overcoat.

"That's it, Rich," he said in his thick Polish accent. "Go ahead, try it on."

I put my arms through the sleeves, buttoned the horn buttons, and stood before the closet's full-length mirror. The coat felt amazing, not like my itchy $14 tweed sports jacket. And it fit perfectly.

Phil watched my every move. I wondered if this might finally be the day when he offered me something.

"Cashmere," he whispered reverentially. "Now put it back in the closet."

He directed me down a flight of narrow, wooden steps to his immaculate basement. Inlaid wood cabinets were filled with French ormolu clocks, marble busts, and other rare *objets d'art*. There were also five glistening black and gold Raleigh racing bikes. My mother had told me that Phil traveled only by bicycle.

"You take the MTA over to Beacon Hill," he said. "I will meet you at 74 Charles Street."

As I walked toward the MTA stop, Phil whizzed past me on one of his Raleighs. When I got to 74 Charles Street, Phil was restlessly sitting on his English bike. He pointed to a black sign with gilt lettering that said "Charles Dana, Jeweler." We went down some metal steps into a long, dimly lit tunnel. I felt like Phil was Boston Blackie, the master jewel thief, and I was his faithful sidekick, The Runt. We came to a heavy, black, lacquered door. Phil rapped a shiny, Turkish, brass, ball-and-claw door knocker. A heavy-set man brought us into a room, wallpapered in black velvet, where elegantly dressed customers, in fur coats and bespoke suits, were perusing glass cases filled with glistening jewelry.

Phil introduced me to Charles Dana and explained my dilemma.

"Richard, I know the situation well," said Dana. "Women are hard to please. But you've come to the right place. Your uncle tells me that your girlfriend has a beautiful charm bracelet."

He opened a showcase and took out a linen-lined tray of charms. There was a gold hatchet, a gold skeleton, a sterling telephone, a silver horse-and-rider with sapphire eyes, and many more. I could barely take them all in.

"Can I see that one?" I timidly asked, pointing to a smiling, bushy-tailed, gold squirrel munching on an acorn.

Dana placed the charm into my hand. I let the squirrel play in my palm as I wondered whether Linda would like it.

"I wouldn't buy that, Richard," Phil interjected. "It doesn't have any craftsmanship. Never, never, never buy anything unless it has craftsmanship. You see that bulldog in the back of the case?"

"Your uncle has good taste," purred Dana as he fetched the dog.

Dana placed the gold bulldog on a soft mat.

"You can see the art," Phil said as we squinted at the 18-carat, half-inch canine. "See the lines in the face? The time and effort the maker put into it?"

The price was exactly the $250 I had in a white envelope. I paid for it gladly, appearing confident it was a wise purchase, but still nervous about Linda's reaction.

The day before her girls-only Sweet Sixteen party, at the Mount Pleasant Country Club, I asked her out to the movies. I picked her up in our Buick Special. As we drove, I tried to gauge her mood. I always had to hitch up her state of mind, as if it were a pair of oversize pants and I were the suspenders.

At the theater, I was eager to get a sneak peek at *Attack of the Giant Leeches,* but I went along with her pick, *Sleeping Beauty.* After the show, when we got back into my car, I pulled out the box. It had a thin blue ribbon tied around it. I thought of this as a dry run to an engagement ring.

"Linda, I got you this present," I said. "Happy birthday." Revealing my insecurity, I added, "I hope you like it."

She didn't kiss me or reach over for a hug—just waited for me to place the box in her hand. After she opened it, she removed the golden bulldog. In the milky streetlight, it looked much more impressive than it did at Charles Dana. I was suddenly confident, convinced, that *craftsmanship* would grab this girl and hold her for me, forever.

"Richard," she began slowly, "this is … very nice. But I don't understand it. What is it?"

I crumbled as she tore in half my entry ticket to her life.

"It's a charm," I explained. "There is a little catch on the bottom for you to hook it on your charm bracelet."

"Oh," she said, still seeming confused. "I can put it on my other charm bracelet, the one that has the less expensive charms."

Now I said, "I don't understand." That's what we say to people when we fully understand but are dumbfounded by their stupidity. Chalk it up to her youth or to her family tradition of shitting on me.

I drove her home, sick to my stomach, though she didn't have a clue.

* * *

I was in recovery from Linda's heart-stomping when I met Connie Smith at a Friday night dance. Connie was sweet—a tall blond; I found her much prettier than Linda, just when I didn't think that was possible. Plus, she didn't have a psycho brother. We liked each other right off and soon we were parking at Bancroft Tower.

She took me home to meet her family, who owned the largest oil and gas company in Central Massachusetts. They could have bought and sold the Pauls and were very kind and hospitable. They lived in a mansion with a much bigger central stairway that had a sculptural newel post. The Smiths belonged to the Worcester Country Club, where no Jew got through the door unless he was making a delivery. Her parents and sisters couldn't have been nicer to me.

Things were going great until the night my dad came into my room and said, "Rich, I heard you've been going out with whores. Is that true?"

He was talking about Connie. My dad was a kind man, but he was extremely naïve and sometimes strangely judgmental. Someone, probably my mother, must have told him I was hanging around with a non-Jewish girl from a bad background. This reverse discrimination messed up my relationship with Connie because we had to sneak around. It was too much for her.

As always, the Crazy Eight provided me solace from girls. We'd play poker after school or drive out to Spencer, a small town outside of Worcester. We'd hang out in the woods near St. Joseph's Abbey, founded a few years earlier by Trappist monks (someone said the monks maintained emotional friendships with each other) seeking solitude in the country. They'd built the famous monastery themselves. We sat there guzzling a case of Pabst Blue Ribbon beer as we watched the monks in their cassocks tend their fields. When our beer ran out, we'd drive down the road to Hot Dog Annie's, a red wooden shack in Leicester. We'd sit in our cars, listening to "Running Bear"—Johnny Preston's song about the doomed romance between an "Indian brave" and a "white girl"—while munching wieners covered with chopped onions and Annie's watery barbeque sauce. We'd head home around 6 p.m.

After a few months at Classical High, my limited patience was really tested. I was haunted by visions of Worcester Academy's commandants, Rader and Piper, drowning me in a vat of vanilla coke at The Spa. My Classical homeroom teacher, Mr. Haggis, was also a hump. He was a handsome, rugged guy who took great pride in his physique. He was fixated on what he considered the "correct" ways of speaking, dressing, and behaving. Often, he found me lacking.

"Golub, can't you do anything correctly?" he'd lament.

I found my revenge in a new NBC game show, "Haggis Baggis." The show, which was on in the daytime *and* the nighttime, featured two contestants who tried to identify a photo of a celebrity that was hidden behind a grid of topical categories. (It was kind of a lame precursor to "Jeopardy!") The show included a bonus round where the winner would secretly choose one of two prizes labeled "Haggis" (luxury items) or "Baggis" (cheap utilitarian items). The opponent had to guess which the winner had chosen. I thought that the TV show was hilarious and pretended to be the host. Every day I would order my friends to choose "haggis or baggis"—even though there was no prize and they knew that.

Early one morning in homeroom, I was deeply involved in hosting "Haggis Baggis." I had drawn a grid and had a picture of a movie star behind it. I asked my friend Slobby Robby to name the star. Before Slobby could answer, I heard Mr. Haggis say, "Golub, what the hell are you doing?"

"Just playing a little 'Haggis Baggis,'" I explained.

"Just a little *what*?" he said. Apparently, he was not familiar with the game that was sweeping the nation, or at least the halls of Classical.

He ordered me to step forward to his desk.

"Are you making fun of my name?" he asked. "My family name is Haggis, not Haggis Baggis!"

I seemed to have touched a nerve. I didn't know then that haggis was an ancient Scottish pudding made of sheep organs cooked in the animal's stomach. It would have been hard to decide what was more disgusting—the dish or this teacher. Maybe he'd been teased about his name even before the game show.

By now, he was literally in my face. We were so close the lapel of his wooly jacket almost touched my nose. I protectively put my hands between us— accidentally causing Mr. Haggis to fall backward over his desk and onto the floor.

No one said anything. We couldn't see behind his desk. For several long seconds he didn't get up. I thought he might have hit his head. Finally, he arose.

"Golub!" he screamed. "Get out of my class! Get out and go to the principal's office!"

It seems that Haggis had fainted. I later found out he was prone to fainting spells.

Once again, I walked the plank to the principal's office.

"You struck a teacher," the principal alleged. "That is unacceptable behavior at Classical. You are permanently expelled."

I'd now been ejected from four schools, if you count the time I was booted out of Chandler for throwing a paper airplane into my math teacher's bouffant.

There were other public high schools in Worcester. I could move on to one of those, perhaps getting thrown out of each one successively. But that seemed like a lot of work. No truant officers were calling my parents to demand that I re-enroll. It was late November and, with the holidays approaching, my mom and dad decided to let me hang around the house.

One of my mother's holiday specialties was her famous extra dry turkey. She used a little white-and-red cooking timer, winding it to the maximum hours, to make sure everything was desiccated. There was never any gravy that might serve as a lubricant. Her turkey left our guests breathless—and searching for anything to wash down the Styrofoam poultry.

Her cooking skills didn't stop my mother from inviting strangers from far and wide. Many were exchange students at Worcester Tech or Worcester State College, where she held office jobs. Coming from countries like Bulgaria and Romania, they usually had unpronounceable names, bony features, and dark circles under their eyes. The girls had long black hair with streaks of gray, even though they were teenagers. They looked undernourished—in other words, perfect customers for my mother's cuisine.

As Thanksgiving led to Christmas, I wandered around Worcester, looking at the decorations on Main Street and the mangy reindeer in Green Hill Park, Worcester's hilly public space, wondering where I'd go to school next.

I was running out of options. On the North Side of Worcester was the creatively named North High. The girls there were mostly well-scrubbed, freckled Catholics who wore beige knee socks and long skirts and only wanted to go out with the Irish quarterback. The school colors were gold and black. I didn't like the students there because they acted like a superior race.

The Worcester School Department preferred that I enter South High. I wasn't crazy about it, either. I didn't like the red and white school colors. The South girls tended to be thick and squat, wore too much red lipstick, and favored short, overweight linemen.

A civil war raged between North and South—though they were united in their hatred of Classical. What was left was Commerce High. Dirty Art went there now, having been expelled from Classical, along with Slobby Robby, after they threatened a female teacher too close to an open window. Art was more comfortable at Commerce, where he said the girls were *voluptuous*. He liked that word after I found it in my *Word Wealth*. But

Commerce was basically a vocational school where you learned how to be a sheet metal worker or an electrician or a plumber. I couldn't see myself showing up at Linda's in a Craftsman tool belt.

CHAPTER 7:

Finding Hell on Earth

I was tempted to quit school altogether. But I felt I should go to college. To get into a decent college, I still figured I needed to go to private school. But what private school would let me in with my transcript?

I found the answer in the waiting room of my dentist. Dr. Griffin, who looked like the actor Gig Young, was always drilling my perfectly fine teeth—talking my mother into paying for more fillings. My mouth was his gold mine. But Dr. Griffin did have good magazines and a bad complexion. It was in the back pages of Argosy or Popular Mechanics where I saw an ad for Brewster Free Academy, a coeducational boarding school in Wolfeboro, New Hampshire.

The school was founded in 1820, which sounded suitably preppy. The word "free" bothered me. Prep schools weren't supposed to be free. Would I be able to tell my friends that I went to an expensive school? As it turned out, Brewster was free only for locals. Students from outside Wolfeboro had to pay tuition. It didn't amount to much money for a rich person, but it would be a struggle for my dad.

Nevertheless, he said I could apply. So, I filled out the one-page application, using my father's store address. I didn't want my mother to know that I was trying to go away to school. My father and I kept it a secret.

A few days later, I received a letter of acceptance; shortly before the semester was due to start, my dad told my mom I was leaving home. She freaked out, yelling that we'd done this behind her back and, once again, I was a son of a bitch. She was half right, but I couldn't stay home any longer. What was I going to do in Worcester? Play cards every day? (I didn't have any money!) Wait for Linda to give me an audience? My mother and I were not getting along. She was at her wits' end by then. She shook her head every time she looked at me. I still don't know where I got the guts to go to a strange place, where I knew no one, in the dead of winter.

Shortly after New Year's 1958, my father and I got into the car and started driving north through a tunnel of snow. I could barely see over the white banks of the two-lane road. The high winds whistled through the car windows. The wipers scratched back and forth on the icy windshield. My dad was silent. I knew he felt very sorry for me. This was just like the day I was kicked out of Worcester Academy. Now I was kicking myself into the middle of a wilderness. Was that progress? I should have been happy to finally be going to a real boarding school. But as we rounded the traffic circle in Portsmouth, New Hampshire, the reality thickened that I wouldn't be seeing Worcester for a long time. Was it too late to back out?

We arrived in the darkness at around 6 p.m. The wind-battered town sign announced "Wolfeboro— Settled 1768." Even in this blizzard I could see that nothing much had changed since then. We parked, and I got out my little, worn, green suitcase. We navigated the maze of shoveled walkways across the Brewster campus. All the snow in New Hampshire couldn't conceal the dreariness of the place. It looked like a down-market version of WA.

We found our way to the white Colonial house where Headmaster C. Richard Vaughn lived with his family. Their living room looked remarkably like the office of Headmaster Piper at WA. I felt like I was being hurled back to square one. Vaughn was less headmasterly than Piper—a nearly friendly style. He had a pale complexion and a rubbery nose. As I studied the precisely combed part of his jet-black hair, Vaughn remarked that he knew Piper. He also revealed that he knew I'd been tossed out of WA and other schools. Vaughn introduced us to his blond wife and his beautiful blond daughter, Jana. "The perfect Aryan family," I remarked to myself. I was already wary of what might happen to a Jew boy in these tractor-torn boondocks.

Vaughn said to my father, "Charles, it would be best if you left Richard at the dining hall. The boarding students are about to have dinner. He could get to know some of them right away."

"All right," my dad answered naively.

"And Charles," Vaughn went on, "does Richard play any sports?"

"Richard is a very good basketball player," my dad replied proudly. "We have a hoop at the end of our driveway, and he is a good shooter."

I appreciated the plug, though Dad knew little about my high school performance or that once, at Newton Square, I'd miraculously beaten Boston Celtic Togo Palazzi, an All-American, one on one—21 to 17.

"We have an excellent basketball team," said Vaughn. "Our top players are named Rice and Bean. BFA is very sports-minded." (That was an understatement—the place practically reeked of athlete's foot.)

"We have an extensive PG program," he went on.

"PG?" my dad asked. "What's that?"

"PGs are postgraduates—guys who didn't finish high school, or who've been out for a few years. Some have served in the military. The government pays their tuition."

My humble dad didn't mention his own World War II heroism.

"I just want to make sure that Richard has a warm room, a good education, and someone to watch over him," Dad said.

"He will be well taken care of; I promise you that" were the headmaster's famous last words.

My stomach sank as the reality of Dad's departure set in. I've said that the fifties were not a decade for hugging, and my father respected that restraint. He conveyed his emotional goodbye with a simple caring look.

I watched his car until the taillights faded from view. Then I walked up the wooden steps of the Estabrook Dining Hall, a three-story white building with a mansard roof and front porch. Its soft lights were welcoming. But as I marched into a room filled with over 100 strangers, it felt like I'd just stepped back outside—the looks were that cold. Students and faculty watched me search for an empty seat. No one smiled or introduced himself. I stood in the middle of the room while they dissected the alien. In Worcester, when someone stared at you, you normally demanded, "What the *fuck* are you looking at?" I figured that probably wasn't the best riposte at that moment. I had to go with the flow. No one told me when you enroll at midterm there is a huge adjustment period.

But who were these people I was adjusting to? They certainly didn't look like a bunch of preppies from rich New England families. They obviously had never heard of Worcester's Ware Pratt and its world-renowned $14 tweed sports jackets, or the House of Doherty around the corner, where I bought snappy silk ties. These guys wore olive drab T-shirts, chinos, sneakers, and black leather boots. Their fashion consultant must have been Dickie's. Did I miss the turn and wind up in a maximum-security prison?

I continued my search for a seat in an elevated alcove flanked by bay windows. There, sitting at six round tables, were older, bigger students. These were the PGs—some of them just out of the Korean War.

"Hey, asshole," one of them yelled, "what's your name?"

Back then, "asshole" was a big insult. It created a picture of the rectum and my ass and all the things that pass through that aperture. In Massachusetts, if someone called you an "asshole," you had to clock them or trade insults—otherwise your self-respect was gone. My dad was too far down the road to rescue me. I was suddenly thrust back to Worcester, back to the fights on Marcy Street, back to the brawl on Newton Square. It was Tatnuck redux. It was like Joseph Conrad's message in *Victory: An Island*: If you run a thousand miles away from your problems, they will show up on your new doorstep and kill you. Now I was standing in my tightly buttoned, food-stained, green winter coat facing a squadron of shell-shocked ex-G.I.'s armed with forks and knives. They wanted to know my name.

In a calm, composed voice, I answered, "John Doe."

Everyone laughed; even I cracked a smile. For a moment I had the impression that I had made a lot of friends, just like the night I performed at the Burwicks. But then one of the PGs, the one who apparently had called me an "asshole," stood up and shouted, "You stupid fuck, I ought to beat the shit out of you!"

It was a ridiculous proposition. Why did he feel the need to beat the shit out of me, as though he were beating the dust out of a Persian carpet? What would he do with all the shit? Nevertheless, pink-skinned, leathery, shorthaired Jim Edgerly was coming for me.

A male teacher came over, put his arm around my shoulder, and waved Edgerly off. He led me to his table, where I ate chicken and drank a glass of cold milk. The teacher told me not to pay attention to Edgerly. It was good advice, but Edgerly was going to pay attention to me. I would grow to despise him like no one I'd ever met.

After dinner, the kind teacher guided me to my dorm, Brown Hall, a brick Georgian building surrounded by tall cypress trees. I climbed four flights to the top floor—a converted attic. My dusty, unlit room had a slanted ceiling that forced you to duck—as though you were always expecting someone to hit you, which I usually was. As I hunched down to enter, I felt like I was walking into a bank vault I'd be locked in for a year.

I did have some company. My new roommate, Jack Payntar, instantly illustrated Jean-Paul Sartre's observation that "Hell is other people." He was about six-foot-four, 250 pounds, and wore a gray sweat suit with BREWSTER emblazoned, in maroon, across his chest. Hailing from Scituate, Massachusetts, he was one of those goddamn postgrads—a baby-faced thug.

"You fucked with my buddy Edgerly," he snorted. "He is going to kick your ass, John Doe."

My dining hall line did seem to amuse him. He chuckled perniciously, "John Doe—that *was* a good one!" This so-called person then announced he was going to be my protector.

"Buddy, I am going to be your fucking pal. I will look out for you!"

Then his large, fat paw slapped my back so hard I flew across the room. I crashed against the dormer window, a spot I would come to know well as I looked out of this cell.

I next met the other three occupants of the fourth floor—all PGs.

Alexander Kravchuk, from Peabody, Massachusetts, had been recently discharged from the United States Army. He looked like his name sounded—a muscular specimen, someone who didn't talk about the past. Although he was in his mid-twenties, he had the dark qualities of an older, buzz-cut Dostoevsky character. He wore khaki pants—they may have been part of his Army uniform—which he kept hitched just below his chest. Kravchuk regularly beat on me. He didn't know when to stop. There wasn't a time I ever saw him in a fight with anyone his own size.

Kravchuk's roommate was a guy named Carpenter. He was equally menacing, in a strangely overt way. He had the broad shoulders of a black-smith who had never seen the light of day—a man who knew only his hammer, an anvil, and intense heat. Carpenter harbored deep-seated anger toward me. Down the hall was another PG named Harry Vedrani, a Navy vet, who had blond hair and a maniacal laugh. Whenever Vedrani whacked me (nearly every time he saw me) he grinned.

The three of them used me as a punching bag.

Across the hall lived 250-pound Frank Santarpio. He was over six feet tall and, inexplicably, called everyone "Cushalino," for which there is no translation. His family had run South Boston's famous Santarpio's bar since 1903. Like the rest of our floor's PGs, Santarpio attended Brewster just to play football. He, too, was older than your typical high schooler. In fact, the 1959 team photo looked like the reunion of college players ten years after graduation. Santarpio was a tackle. He was rough on the field but good-natured and never messed with me.

My first night in Brown Hall's dark fourth-floor attic was not unpleasant. Payntar even asked me where I was from. But the next day, after school, my would-be protector locked me in the clothes closet, snickering as I begged him to let me out. Then he went off to the gym, leaving me imprisoned. I finally managed to use one of his cleated football shoes to hack my way through the closet's wooden door panels.

Payntar and my other floor-mates were like the virulent petals of a black flower. Wherever the wind blew their seeds, weeds grew.

It didn't take long to figure out that Brewster was not really a school. It was an institution that permitted the so-called students who I always viewed as inmates to roam the grounds, much like they would at a clinic or a hospital. The so-called faculty were apparently guards dressed in civilian clothes.

The postgraduates—and there were many of them—impersonated students. Their facial parts barely moved. A nose, an eye, a mouth, a cheek seemed mechanized, rigid zones. Smiles materialized concomitant with the infliction of pain produced by many of them.

Most of Brewster's courses seemed designed so that no one could fail. In my first semester, my physics class required only that we walk down to Lake Winnipesaukee every day at 11 a.m. to take the temperature of the water. My English teacher used elementary-level grammar books I'd used at May Street School. The girls basketball coach, John B. Nay, taught mechanical drawing. Mr. Rogers incarnate, he was a reserved man, who just happened to look like a rusting T-square. I was never good at drawing, printing, or even signing my name. But it didn't seem to matter to Mr. Nay. When I handed him my drawing, he flashed a toothless smile and put my draft in a thin cardboard box. He never commented on the work. He was rumored to have a clapboard house filled with bales of ungraded drafting assignments.

After school, when I didn't have an activity, I went to my attic dungeon, where I'd find Payntar lying on his bed in his boxer shorts and sweaty white T-shirt. I'd try to make friendly conversation. But that didn't stop him from beating the shit out of me or locking me in the clothes closet. I cannot explain why I never complained to anyone in Brewster's administration or went to the cops. Maybe it was because there was no one to complain to.

Wolfeboro billed itself as "The Oldest Summer Resort in America." Many wealthy and famous people—like newlyweds Prince Rainier and Princess Grace—visited the lake when it was warm. But there was nothing much to do in winter. Yes, the school had a rope-tow small ski slope, but I didn't take advantage of it. It would have been difficult to avoid the PGs' savagery, who bashed and crashed into other skiers.

The town itself was sleepy. I couldn't justify spending my free time hanging around the petrol pumps or hardware store, chewing the fat about weed killer, shotguns, and work boots. Maybe it was because I was homesick, but I was drawn to the grocery store, Stinchfield's. Old man Stinchfield had a handsome, blond daughter named Bonnie who went to Brewster. Bonnie was the junior prom queen and a member of the Tri-Hi-Y. She wrote in my 1960 yearbook that I was "a study hall pest," but generously added, "You will reach your goal with little effort."

I did make the basketball team, but I sat on the bench for the entire season. The tweed-jacketed coach, Edward Murphy, was a narcissistic, pompous jerk who claimed he could recall everything that had happened every day of his life. In fact, he could do just that. I tested him, asking what happened on my birthday when I saw him that day. He vividly recalled the events of that day with precision. A true man who had the gift of hyperthymesia.

Headmaster Vaughn must have known that five days a week at Brewster was the mental limit. So, unlike many private schools, the academy let students spend weekends away from campus. I would do anything to get away from the fourth floor of Brown Hall. And, obviously, I wanted to see Linda. There were no direct trains or buses to Worcester, which was two hours away by car. So, I had to hitchhike.

I sometimes waited for hours for a single car to pass by. One weekend, in February 1959, a driver gave me a lift about ten miles outside Wolfeboro. Hoping for another ride, I stood on a cold and windy bend that banked like a racetrack. It was hard to maintain my balance on the icy pavement, or to see oncoming traffic. For several hours underdressed, I shivered there with my hands in my pockets. Finally, I passed out in the dark.

I woke up on the third floor of Huggins Hospital in Wolfeboro. I still don't know how I got there. The nurse at my bedside said, "Richard, you have pneumonia. You will be here for several days. You are very weak. You nearly froze to death on the highway."

I tried to respond, but I'd lost my voice. I fell back to sleep. Over the next few days, I drifted in and out of consciousness as I struggled to breathe. One day, my convalescence was ruptured when I opened my eyes to find the nightmarish specter, Jim Edgerly. That rube stood over my bed, scowling at me, like a blinding spotlight. Then he started rapidly punching me in the stomach and face.

"Who the fuck is John Doe now?" he demanded to know. "Who the fuck is John Doe now?"

I just couldn't answer him at that moment— though I later remembered that "John Doe" was the name a coroner would write on the toe tag of an unidentified corpse, which I was on my way to becoming, thanks to Edgerly.

Thankfully, a nurse walked in and pulled him off me. The next day I woke up with huge bruises on my face that felt like small trumpets. I was black and blue all over.

I spent so much time at the hospital that, after I recovered, I got a part-time job there as an orderly. It paid $30 a week. I disposed of items that would clearly be classified now as toxic waste. I also disposed of bodily fluids I hadn't known existed. Of course, I didn't tell Linda about any of that.

The hospital became a refuge for me. I found friends there. The nurses and the doctors were cordial and considerate and so inspiring that, for a moment, I thought I would go to medical school. I was changing careers in my head based on my ever-evolving circumstances. I kept thinking I was doing nothing with my life while fourteen-year-old Bobby Fischer was winning the U.S. chess championship.

There were too many hair-raising incidents at Brewster that year to recall. The school was a Darwinian laboratory where your ability to survive was tested daily. There was a real possibility I wouldn't get out of there alive. Who knew how many of my predecessors were resting prematurely in Wolfeboro's Lakeview Cemetery?

The north shore of Massachusetts sent Brewster some of its most bestial sons—for instance, Bill Kelleher and his best friend, Jim O'Keefe, both from Lynn. They both had shaved heads and wore the same clothes.

They routinely stole clothes, watches, sneakers, and sports equipment from other students. Without any stealth, they'd then put a price tag on each item and offer it for sale in the "store" they operated out of their dorm room. If a guy wanted his jacket back, Kelleher and O'Keefe were only too happy to sell it to him.

Their hard-knock logic extended to the sports field. In the spring of '58, Brewster's baseball team was playing Tilton Academy at home. I was sitting next to Kelleher and O'Keefe in the bleachers. It was the seventh inning and Tilton's pitcher had a no-hitter going. O'Keefe said to Kelleher, "I'll fix this." He climbed down from the bleachers, ambled out to the pitcher's mound and, in front of an astonished crowd, cold-cocked Tilton's hurler. Game over.

Esta and me in 1944 while my dad was fighting the Nazis in Italy

My dad when Rome was liberated June 5, 1944

My dad around age 18 in front of The Green Street Market

My father's store. I grew up on the second floor until I was ten.

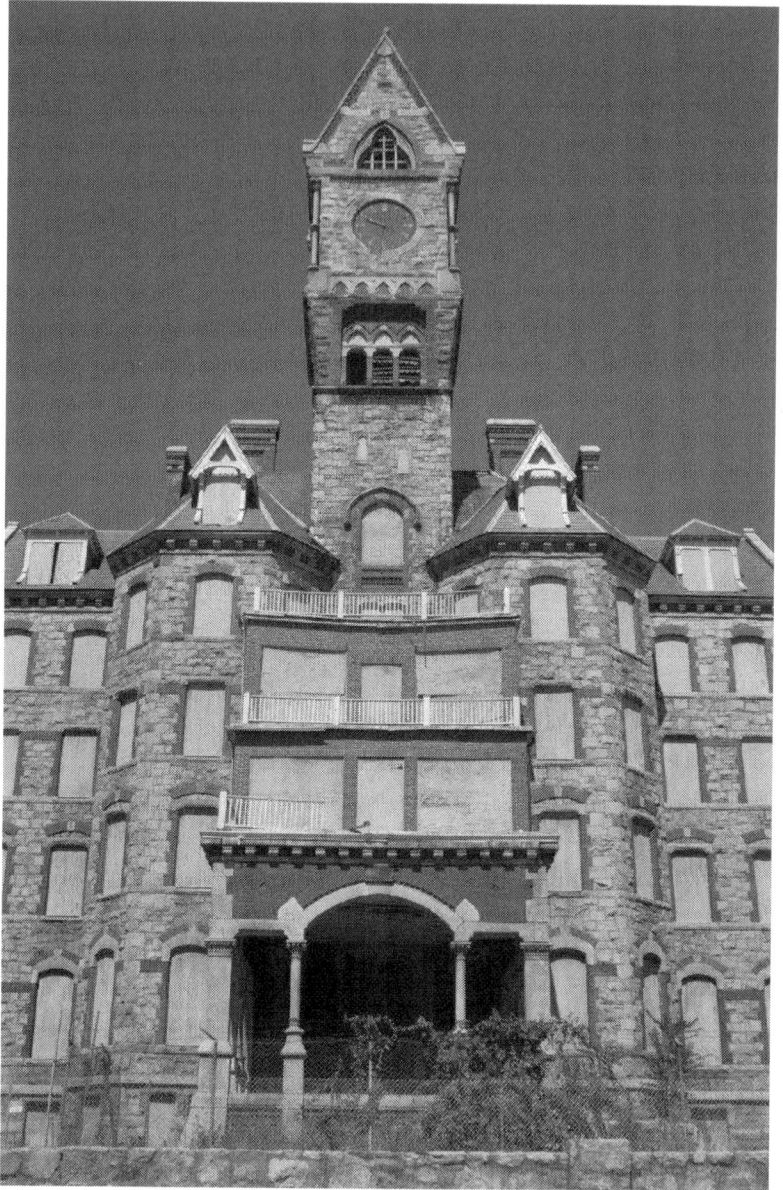

Worcester State Hospital, Department of Mental Health

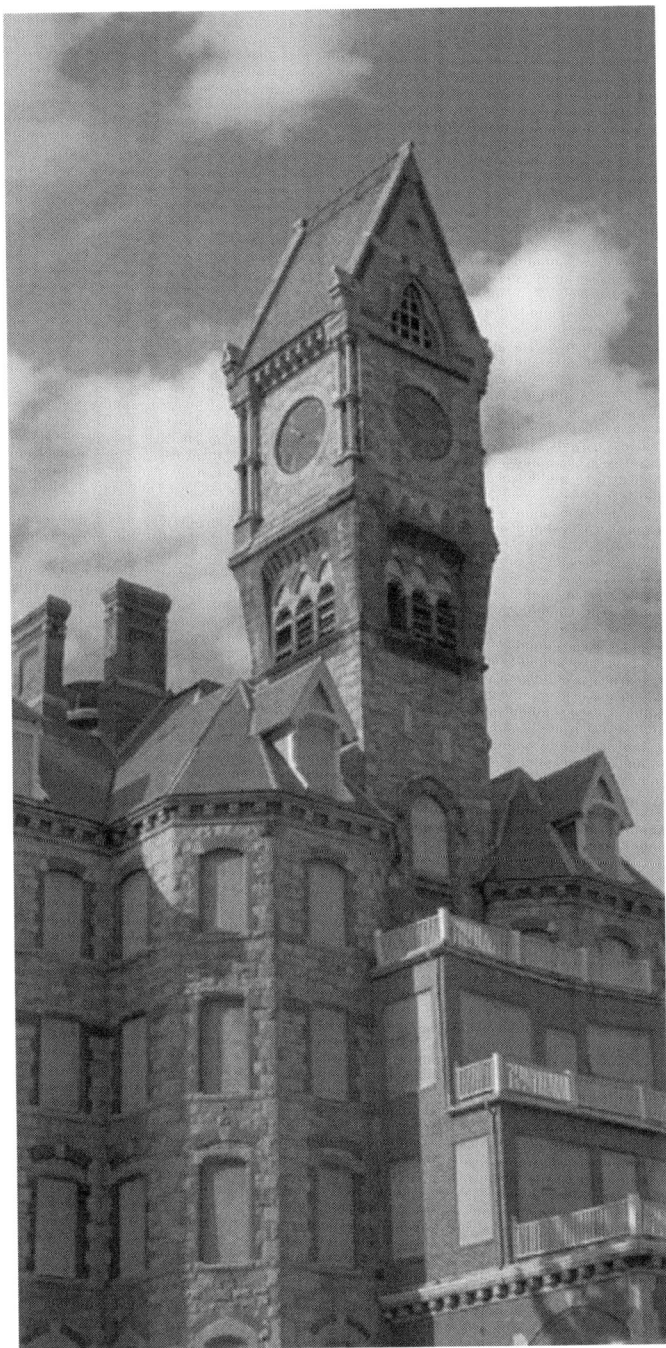

Another view of what we called the nut house.

Another view of Worcester State Hospital

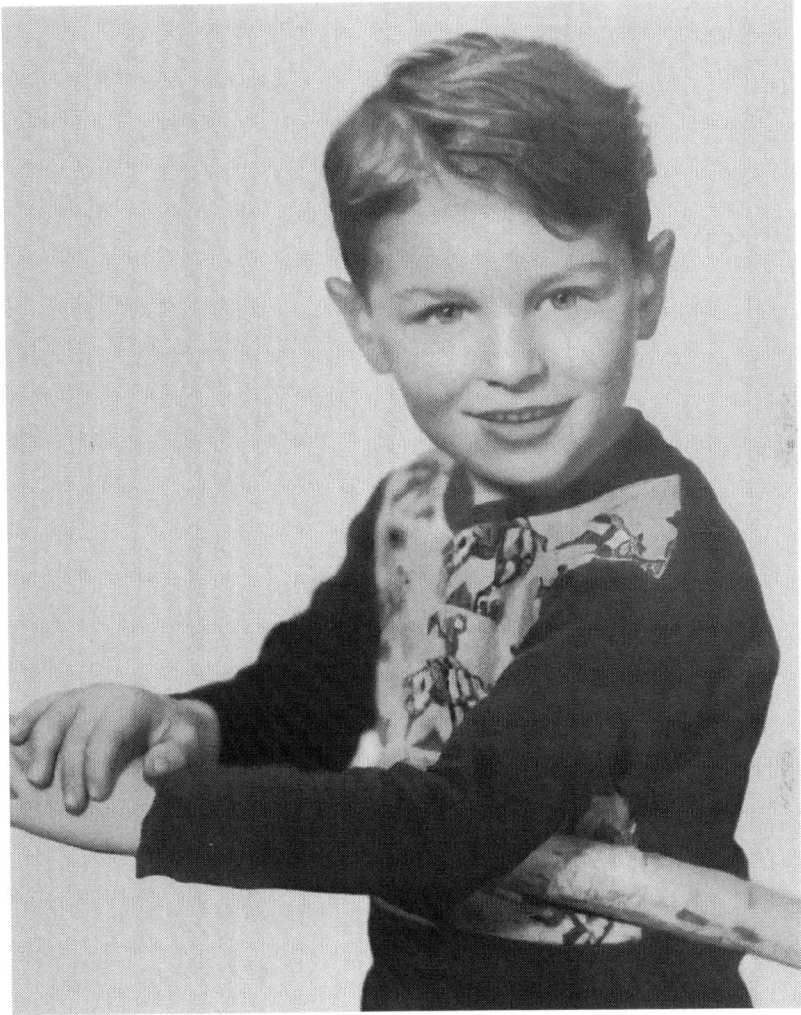

Innocent me, age eight

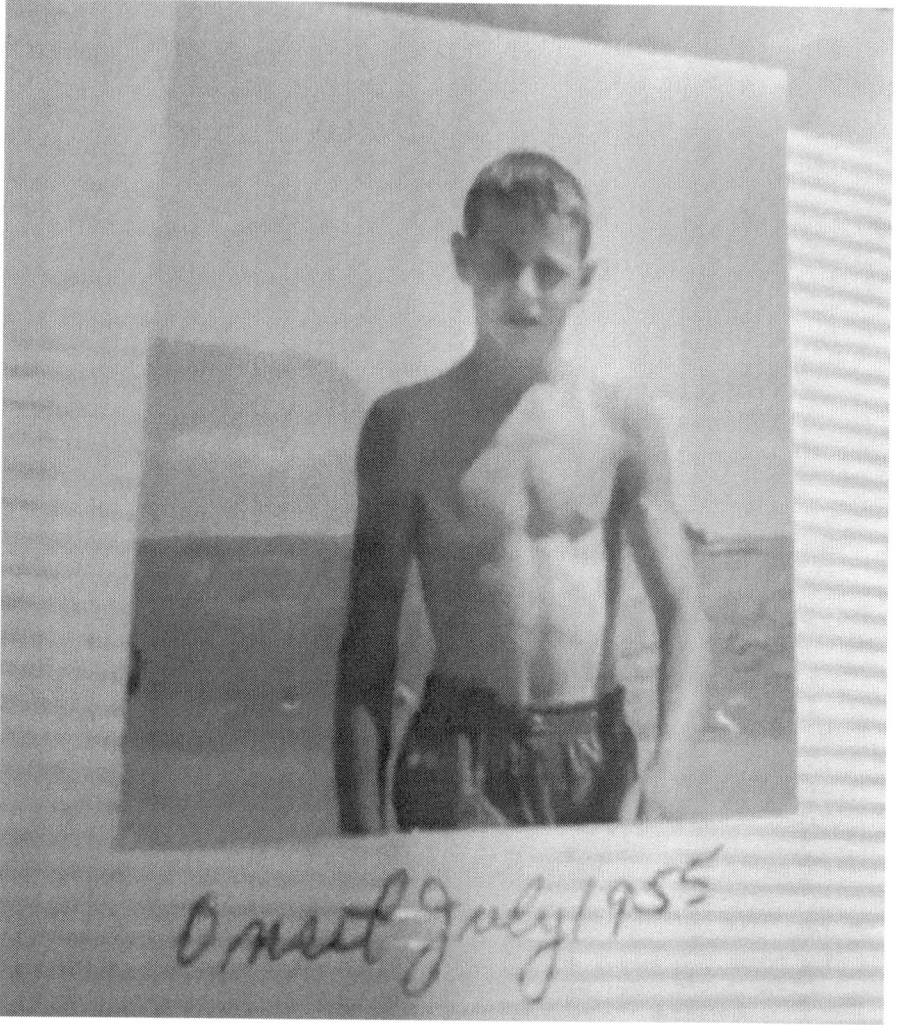

Age twelve at Onset Beach, Cape Cod

Age fourteen with unknown dog in the backyard

A bad photo of Linda Paul

Me and my pals at Brewster Academy, 1960

First year at Umass, not a great place to send your kid

Graduation from Clark University, 1965

CHAPTER 8:

Finishing What I Started

I made it to June at Brewster, completing my junior year. I returned to Worcester. Linda was away at camp in Maine. It wasn't until late August that she arrived home in her linen shorts. I must have spent half of each day waiting by the phone. When we finally met, she acted *aloof*—an adjective *Word Wealth* had supplied, early on, to describe her behavior. I was constantly measuring the distance between us, always picturing her standing on the distant side of an enormous sunlit meadow. No matter how I waved my arms or yelled her name she never turned to look at me. Even in my fantasy I was in denial, telling myself it could have been the whistling wind or the blinding sun that kept her from responding.

Ever since I met her, I knew there was an imbalance in the way we felt about each other. That August, Linda admitted she'd been seeing other guys. She said her mother wanted her to see a lot of different boys. She maintained that she hadn't kissed any of them. She insisted that she was interested only in me. But she would never say she loved me. She'd only commit to "I like you." What the fuck was that? I was carrying around a boulder of emotion in my stomach with her name painted on it. If that wasn't love, then what the hell was it? I began to sense a denouement in the making, and it was not going to go in my favor.

One of the guys she'd seen was Joel Robbins. For Chrissakes, Joel was a member of the Crazy Eight! Like a brother! When I confronted him, Joel swore Linda had made the first move, but nothing happened. He didn't find her that interesting or beautiful. Maybe that's why Joel later became my best friend.

One afternoon, during a poker game at Slobby Robby's, Dirty Art said he'd heard Linda had plans that night to see another guy—Albert Tapper, younger brother of Charlie Tapper, who'd whupped Toastie Santos. Albert went to Classical with Linda. He was intelligent, good-looking, and stood well over six feet. (I never made it beyond five-foot-eleven—another of my childhood gripes.) Like Charlie, Albert strutted around Newton Square in his tennis whites. He was the type that the Pauls would invite to lunch at the Mount Pleasant Country Club. They might even offer him more than one black olive.

Art told me, "I have my cousin Shelly's Buick Roadmaster tonight. We can use her car to follow them. They would recognize your car or mine."

I was dying to see Linda. If I couldn't go out with her, the next best thing was watching her with another guy.

"Great," I said. "I can spy on them to see if they're making out."

"Arbo," Dirty Art said under his breath.

Around 8 o'clock, we spotted Linda and Albert in his black Pontiac convertible. We began tailing them around town, staying about twenty feet behind. We followed them to the movies. We were even going to buy tickets and observe them from the balcony, but we decided instead to stay in the car, like cops on a stakeout waiting for the two love criminals to emerge. Based on the suspects' time of arrival, we determined they were seeing *Auntie Mame*. It was a choice that foreshadowed Albert's later career as an Off-Broadway composer, lyricist, and playwright. I would've taken Linda to *The Blob*, starring Steve McQueen, which was playing at the other end of Main Street.

For two hours, I suffered as I pictured Linda and Albert French-kissing, licking popcorn butter off one another's fingers, not even watching the movie. Finally, they came out with the crowd. They paused under the marquee and—shit—they were holding hands! Linda looked beautiful and happy as hell without me.

They got into Albert's Pontiac. We shadowed them through Worcester. It looked like they were headed to Bancroft Tower! But just when I thought Albert was going to take the turn, he drove straight. Thank God they were not going "parking." I was champing at the bit, in the passenger's seat of Shelly's Buick, trying to see into Albert's convertible, looking for any sign that Linda was faithful to me. It was hard to see her in the clear, but I could tell she was sitting close to Albert, and he had his long arm around her.

As they drove up Kensington Road, I was feeling better and better about the love of my life. Like a nice guy, Albert was taking her home—take the girl to the movies and then drive her straight home to her parents. It was around midnight. Art and I drove around the other way to the top of her street. We were discreetly parked about 100 feet from where Albert and Linda had pulled up in front of Linda's house. Now Dirty Art and I had a clear view of what they were doing—and what they were doing was... furiously making out! I could feel my heart beating out of my chest. I had solid, undeniable proof that she was unfaithful.

Then, suddenly, they stopped kissing. The driver's door of the Pontiac flew open. Albert got out and marched straight toward Dirty Art and me. I ducked under the glove compartment. Dirty Art jumped into the back and laid down on the floor. Tapper's footsteps came closer and closer before I heard his knuckles rap on the windshield, then the passenger's window.

"Golub, you stupid fuck," he said loudly. I didn't move. Then he was gone. I heard his footfalls as he marched back down Kensington Road. Dirty Art got up in the back.

"Itsy, Tapper outsmarted us—you have to admit," Dirty Art cracked. "Arbo!"

I got up and looked out the dirty windshield. They were standing on the front steps of her house, and the bastard was giving her a long good-night kiss. It seemed to go on forever. Albert looked up at the Buick. We ducked again. The next time I glanced up, Albert's Pontiac was gone. The light was on in Linda's room—the pink room. This was a far cry from the times I spent in her room. It was now a memory. I would never be invited into the pink pleasure palace again.

* * *

Some positive things happened that summer, if you want to call my interest in the law a high point.

Beneath our house was a dank basement. The stairway down was lined with canned goods and cleaning supplies. It wasn't a knotty pine basement like the Pauls' finished rec room. But its walls were paneled with ugly beaver board—compressed wood fiber—and it had black-and-white floor tiles like the Pauls' place. Most importantly, around the corner from the laundry room and across from the noisy boiler, it had a 29-inch built-in Admiral black-and-white TV set. I watched sports and movies there, usually alone. While Linda was painting away in her posh basement thinking of New York and Picasso and her rosy future, I was studying the histrionics of the legal profession. *Witness for the Prosecution*, starring Charles Laughton, Marlene Dietrich, and Tyrone Power, first got me interested in courtroom drama. That's where I grossly misunderstood myself. I really wanted to be an actor. But, in Worcester, lawyers topped the list of respectable people.

I wanted to overcompensate for my dad's struggle in the grocery business. Although I wouldn't feel this way now, I was ashamed of what my dad did for a living, because he didn't get the respect he deserved. *He* didn't give a damn. All he cared about, besides our family, were his customers. By becoming a lawyer, I could pull the entire family up and remove dad's bloody butcher's apron. Everyone in Worcester would look at us differently. I now see those two jobs as one and the same. Legal papers and groceries are both carried in cardboard boxes. The client is the customer.

Party Girl was the film that clinched my legal destiny. Released in 1958, it starred Robert Taylor, Cyd Charisse and Lee J. Cobb. I wanted to screw Cyd Charisse and be Robert Taylor. Taylor played mob lawyer Tommy Farrell. In the movie, Tommy dresses beautifully in a dark three-piece double-breasted suit, complete with a Marcella waistcoat. He has a gimpy leg. In the courtroom, he limps from the counsel table to the jury box and hands Juror #1 his antique cane. Then he gingerly places his gold pocket watch on the wooden railing. He begins his opening statement by saying, "My grandfather gave me this watch. Keeps good time. I won't waste yours during this case." The pocket watch stays there, throughout the trial, ticking away every day.

That was it for me. I knew I was going to be a star litigator. Only a year before, I'd been tossed out of WA. But now I was on the straight and narrow—dedicated to vindicating my beleaguered father, even if it meant forcing my wild character into a mold and sticking my nose into moldy law books.

My mother didn't believe me when I said I was going to become an attorney at law. She continued her mantra: "You could really please me by becoming an accountant—or just graduating from high school." That summer, I worked for the accounting firm of Feingold and Feingold, putting little numbers in small square migraine-inducing boxes. Of course, I didn't tell Linda I worked in an accounting firm and was paid $1.25 an hour. Nor did I tell her that I was fantasizing about screwing Cyd Charisse as soon as I finished screwing Anita Ekberg and Elizabeth Taylor.

After the summer, I returned to Brewster. My dad drove me, once again, up Routes 16 and 11, now snowless, as we wended our way back to the source of my misery. He and I seemed to have had a better time on this trip. I didn't know exactly what the year would hold but I knew that motley crew from the fourth floor of Brown Hall had graduated, and I wouldn't see them ever again.

Wolfeboro slowly materialized in the distance— looking like a New England hamlet where you might lodge overnight, snug under a colorful, hand-quilted duvet, then wake up to shirred eggs, sausages, and rye toast. Quaint as shit! Wolfeboro felt surprisingly comfortable. The air was cool. I loved the smell of the trees and the campus' freshly mowed lawn. For the first time, I took in the view of the lake from the knoll next to Estabrook Hall. I exhaled like a grizzly bear. The scene was breathtaking. Why didn't I ever notice it before?

The first night I went to dinner that semester I felt fearless and clear-headed. There was none of that "John Doe" business. Maybe Headmaster Vaughn had weeded out the bullies. Everyone was starting fresh, and the mood was uplifting.

I was assigned a room in Furber House, a whitewashed, shingled, architecturally deficient, three-story dwelling that had once been some family's home. It felt like the original owners had never moved. Once again, the school had stuck me in the attic. My roommate under the sloped wainscot ceilings was the inexcusably jovial Gordon Rule Tyke Lee. He claimed that he was a direct descendant of Robert E. Lee. Inasmuch as he was from Manchester, New Hampshire, had a round face and husky build, and didn't look in any way like the Confederate general, I was sarcastic toward him from Day One. I called him "General," or "Tyke," never Gordon. He loved it when I snapped to attention and called him "The General."

Gordon studied every night, under a rusted chrome lamp at a little desk on the opposite side of the room. He required absolute quiet so he could "concentrate." Well, of course. Everyone wanted to concentrate. Everyone was trying to comb away their problems with their families, their girlfriends, their money issues, their feuds with the other students, their athletic inability, their indigestion from the shitty Brewster food, and to focus on the bicameral system of our great government. But other than demanding absolute quiet, The General went along with everything.

The difference between our senior class and the last one was enormous. None of us were violent—though we couldn't resist a few pranks. We used to jump on classmate Ronald Grelli's bed until its slats and springs broke. We did it so many times that Grelli once asked me to kill him. But no one ever touched him. It was all directed at his bed. And not just *his* bed. John Schmidt was a science genius but also a pain-in-the ass snitch. One day we tucked a heavy road construction sign under his covers. When he found it, he said, "Golub, I think you did it," until he found out that my friend, Harry Read, had taken a dump in Schmidt's bed.

I found a new friend in Mike Capone, a short guy with short hair and a small head, from Fitchburg, Massachusetts. Mike claimed he was a distant cousin of Chicago mob boss Al Capone. (Untrue.) Mike took nothing seriously. His personality had many of the playful shades of Dirty Art's. He could rattle off jokes that he'd been memorizing since childhood. I called Mike "Subia," the name of the planet he said was his home. He called me "Subash," which may have been a satellite of Subia. Often, we'd switch our names, just to confuse Earthlings. At night, we terrorized the Furber House kids, banging on their doors and running through their rooms, wearing ratty terry cloth bathrobes backward and plastic dry-cleaning bags braced by metal coat hangers.

"We are from Subia," we screamed.

Harry Read was a good-humored, muscular fullback, who assisted us, like with Schmidt's bed. Harry was not from Subia, although he desperately wanted to be. (The following year, Harry wound up in the same college dorm as my nemesis, Jim Edgerly. Harry claimed he took it upon himself to beat the shit out of Edgerly on my behalf.)

Despite the torture I endured the year before, I was starting to be seduced and co-opted by Brewster Free Academy. In the fall I played soccer. I remember looming in the goal like a praying mantis. I have no distinct memories of flying across the goal with my arms outstretched. I can't even recall kicking or throwing a soccer ball. But there is a 1960 yearbook photo of me standing with the team and I look like I was part of something I was enjoying.

Aside from joining in school activities, I also created many of my own. My mind was racing a thousand miles an hour to no particular destination. The practice of creating my own entertainment stemmed from my friendless childhood. Now I had accomplices who could help me develop and produce my imagination's odd scenarios.

When I was thirteen, I used to imitate old Jewish grandmothers doing what I called the "Bubby Walk." I would pull my shoulders in, hunch my back, pull a kerchief over my head, and walk down Water Street, where kosher food was sold. The kerchief hid my face, except for my nose, which I constantly scratched as I talked in Yiddish to myself. I also invented a paternal counterpart I called "Zadie's Run" (Zadie being Yiddish for grandfather). Dressed in black clothes and a wide-brimmed black hat, I dragged my feet and jabbered in Yiddish. People young and old would ask me to do the Bubby Walk and the Zadie's Run. (Of course, Linda never knew about them.) I still meet people from Worcester who remember the Bubby Walk and the Zadie's Run and, unfortunately, my peeing out a school window.

So many times, since my early adolescence, I'd wanted to drop everything, take it on the count of three, and dance extemporaneously—no music, no beat, no nothing. Just let the dance do all the talking! Therapeutic dance was my baby way before Dr. Arthur Janov came up with Primal Scream. I didn't take any credit for my brainstorm's relaxing and purgative effects. But, like Dr. Janov, I theorized that every student and faculty member at Brewster suffered from some form of repressed pain. They clearly manifested unfulfilled needs that had to be released. Why shouldn't Brewster be my clinic?

So, I started the C.D.C.—the Crazy Dance Club. The club probably had its foundation in my own need to exorcise my brutal and grotesque Brown Hall demons, to cleanse myself by shaking, twisting, and contorting my body in every way possible. Yes, the club sprang from my will to survive, but I also wanted to help others survive Brewster. Ten guys were charter members. Women were not allowed, not that any appeared to be interested in joining.

Every night we gathered in a small living room outside of the main dining hall. None of us could enter the hall before thanking the prep school gods for the imminent meal by way of free-form movements. These included aggressive arm thrusts, a bit of ass wiggling, and some airborne dry humping. The primary focus was our feet. We had plenty of floor space and we covered it with nonstop stomping, sideway kicks, and anything else our legs could come up with. Our heads also moved—rapidly up and down. There was a Yes Dance and a No Dance. None of the C.D.C members knew any actual choreography. But that didn't prevent the occasional solo in the middle of the room. The Twist was the fad at the time, but no one in New Hampshire knew who the hell Chubby Checker was. It was The Crazy Dance that was taking the hillbilly state by storm.

The C.D.C. had one faculty member, John Coyne. All the other members were in Coyne's history class. Coyne was a thin-haired, stubby man who perspired profusely. He favored black horned-rimmed glasses and a Julius Caesar haircut. He was an excellent teacher, from whom I coincidentally learned about the Roman Empire. In addition, I thought he was a dead ringer for Peter Lorre, one of my favorite actors. Back then, I called everyone I liked "a good man" and Coyne was a prime example of a good man.

How could you not like Coyne, especially after he started the Coin Club? The Coin Club met on Wednesday afternoons, after school, in Coyne's classroom. Coyne knew a lot about numismatics and encouraged each of us to stuff albums with Lincoln pennies and Roosevelt dimes. But we never looked at our coins unless another teacher entered the room. Mostly, we just told dirty jokes and stories about girls we knew. Coyne just listened; I don't think he ever had a girlfriend. He liked goofing around with us.

One night, a bunch of us were playing poker in our Fruit of the Looms, in a different dorm. The game was getting out of hand in a very small room. We didn't have any beer, but we were rowdy—throwing around cards and food. There was some dancing, though not full-out Crazy Dancing. Some of the guys were pissed because they'd lost their allowance. The racket drew the attention of Coyne, who was proctor of that dorm. Another proctor would have shut us down. Not only did Coyne let the mayhem escalate, but he also jumped into the action, stripping down to his white boxers and knee-high socks, held up by garters. His sweaty potbelly shimmered and shook as he tried to dance. Plus, he started throwing food around, including an ice-cold Coca-Cola that sailed into my face. Coyne called himself a "proper Bostonian." He loved to laugh and didn't mind being laughed at. I suppose he may have been trying a little too hard to be one of the boys. But, even late into life, many prep school grads still want to be one of the boys.

That night we welcomed Mr. Coyne into the Crazy Dance Club. I gave him an official C.D.C. Life Membership card, featuring a bearded New Hampshire hillbilly dancing in his overalls. The card was signed by Richard Golub, "Dance Master."

* * *

Not long after that night, I found myself unsatisfied with the Crazy Dance Club. I realized there wasn't any lasting entertainment value in it—except for those few minutes before we sat down for a meal in Estabrook. The members danced energetically and with great sincerity, but there wasn't enough bang for my buck. I felt danced-out and bored.

I had some earnest talks with Mike Capone, aka Subia. He was troubled by my ennui. He was deadly serious about fucking around and acting insane. They were his stock in trade. He and I went for long walks, like two important diplomats, like Aristotle's Peripatetics, pondering a new path forward, something enduringly demented. After weeks of perambulations, we founded The Spell Club.

It had nothing to do with spelling words. No, we were going to cast spells. Our spells would freeze a person in their tracks—wherever they were, day or night, nude or clothed. Our spells lasted as long as we wanted. Thrown properly, the spell must be accompanied by a car siren (which the Spell Club member would simulate). The casting device was a misty, ethereal tool suspended in the sky. It resembled a spinning wheel with a handle. The Spell Club member would crank the handle—first slowly, then faster, as though he were firing up a Model T Ford. When he'd wound the spell spring as tightly as it would go, the member would release the spell at his target. Once a person was hit by the spell, every part of his body was paralyzed. A member could lift the spell by saying, "Lleps" ("Spell," spelled backward) or "Lesp" (because it was easier to say).

The spell could be used to cripple an attacker. Any reason would do. Or no reason. Some days I'd freeze as many as fifteen students around the dorm. They'd hold their poses for ten minutes or more. The ones outside looked like a sculpture garden. I might freeze one person on the campus green, another on Estabrook's wooden steps, still others in the bathroom stalls at Furber House. I found ways to expand the Spellscape around Wolfeboro.

People played along because it was just plain insane. The Spell Club gave me a huge status credit. It was the power boost I desperately needed after my miserable junior year. I was then, and am now, wracked by nervousness, although no one has ever told me, "You look nervous." The Spell Club had a tranquilizing effect on me.

The apex of the Spell phenomenon came around 11 a.m. on a Tuesday. I was walking down the third-floor hallway of the main Academic Building. John Coyne was speaking to Headmaster Vaughn—gesticulating excitedly as usual. As I passed them, my right hand curled into a fist, which I slowly opened. I pointed my fingers at Coyne and whispered, "Spell, Coyne." He stood motionless, closing his mouth in mid-sentence. His fluttering hands went as limp as a plugged quail. Vaughn looked at Coyne as though he'd just suffered a stroke—inspecting him like a piece of tainted beef in a supermarket. Coyne didn't move a muscle, faithful as a Marine to the Spell Club. *Semper fidelis.* In that moment, I knew Coyne was one of a kind. I saw his eyes rotate toward mine. It dawned on me that my spell might be putting his job on the line. But he didn't indicate in the least that I should release him. Finally, against my better judgment, I walked back to Coyne and whispered, "Lleps,"

Turning back at the end of the corridor, I saw Coyne, reinvigorated, talking rapid fire to a befuddled Vaughn. It was one of the best laughs of my life.

The next day I ran into Coyne at breakfast. Stuffed into his scuffed-up oxfords and rumpled black suit, he was moping near a stainless-steel platter of scrambled eggs. While I chewed on a long strip of bacon, he confided that he'd been fired. He had to catch a Greyhound bus.

Walking out the door, he said respectfully, "Richard, you are the Grand Supreme Spell Master."

As he walked toward the bus stop, in front of Furber House, he gazed back at the campus and some students. I waved to him and wondered if my spell had anything to do with his dismissal. But I was a kid and kids have a limited capacity to feel guilty. Only now, as I reflect on Coyne's shiny forehead and endearing smirk, do I see that I had a hand in his departure. Then again, I have no doubt that Coyne enjoyed being a member of our clubs. They weren't fancy clubs like the kind where guys walk around in alpaca sweaters and one leather golf glove. But we entertained each other, and that's more than I can say for most of my connections with faculty.

I heard that Coyne returned to Boston's public school system. Then he vanished into one crowd or another. We lost track of him. If only I'd thrown a grand spell—a spell heard 'round New England—when I'd had the chance. I might have frozen him, like Lot's wife, so that he couldn't leave Brewster, so that Wolfeboro would always have a lifelike statue of him. As it is, I will always be a loyal member of Coyne Club.

About two weeks later, on a weeknight, Mike Capone and I were running around Furber House as Martians—dressed, as usual, in our backward terry cloth bathrobes, plastic dry-cleaning bag spacesuits, and coat hanger antennae. On the first floor, Mike had the bad luck of running right smack into the new Furber House proctor—the guy who'd replaced Coyne. He was walking around like a storm trooper, doing bed checks with none other than sour-faced, needle-nosed Headmaster Vaughn. Through my plastic bag I saw them apprehend Mike. I saw his sad expression, not unlike Coyne's departing glance. I ducked down the corridor behind us, threw my plastic bag and coat hanger in the trash, and dashed up the back steps to my dorm room.

In the morning, I stood in the hall and looked out the open front door. Mike was getting into his mother's car—headed home for a mandatory two-week expulsion. He glared at me, casting an accusing look in my direction. But there was no way this was my fault. Like me, he was as crazy as a high school kid could get. When he returned to Brewster, he avoided me. He didn't attend any of the Spell Club meetings and refused to accept or throw a spell. Forty years after we graduated, I would call him from time to time. I'm still waiting for him to call me back.

* * *

Senior year ended without a graduation ceremony. That didn't bother me. Where would you even find a cap and gown in Wolfeboro? In Stinchfield's frozen food section? Who would have given the commencement address? Maybe a psychiatrist. We all needed one by then. Instead, on our last night, we self-medicated at Bailey's Motel, owned by the family of Alan Bailey—classmate and party gladiator. Most of my friends were there—plastered, emotional, and acting like this was not the end. But it was; I would never see any of them again.

By then, I'd received college acceptance and rejection letters. I didn't apply to any Ivy League schools because my SAT scores were in the mid-500s. Despite my years of studying *Word Wealth*, I didn't get that semantic word-game stuff—"Which word *best* matches why the doctor didn't go to work that day?" In those days they didn't have SAT prep courses, or I didn't know about them. Since I got kicked out of two high schools, and with the inadequate education I was receiving at Brewster, I felt ill-equipped for college. Yet I was accepted to Boston University, the University of Massachusetts, and lots of state schools. For months I hounded my parents to let me go to Boston University. My father was willing, but my mother said we couldn't afford BU's tuition, and she had the bucks. She wasn't going to part with what was left of her inheritance. So, as things stood, I was bound for state college UMass-Amherst.

One reason I was so keen on BU was because that's where Linda wanted to go. Linda was born about ten months after me, so she still had to finish high school. But she had her sights set on BU's Fine and Applied Arts program. Because, lest I ever forget, Linda was an artist, and artists are special people. I must admit, back then, I really didn't know the difference between Picasso and Pinocchio. And by the summer of 1960, I didn't know where I was with Linda. I would tell anyone who asked, "We're going steady," or I'd say "steadily." The latter implied we saw other people. Maybe I should have said "steady as she goes." Any day now I might find her pink princess phone disconnected. I wondered when I would free-fall into the abyss without my Linda. When you're a kid you have a prescience, a sense of how things are going to work, that you can see into the future. You're secure in your assumptions.

But assumption is the enemy of state and of humanity. Assuming I could stalk Linda on a date probably wasn't a good idea. I only drove her back into the arms of Albert Tapper. I heard they'd been out on more dates. The grapevine also revealed she'd been stepping out with other non-Crazy Eight acquaintances of mine. My imagination became a twenty-four-hour grindhouse theater that played a stag film showing strange guys kissing Linda, dialing up her small breasts, making her nipples stand at attention, at which point she'd say, "Hold it, I am still a virgin."

That summer I tried to take my mind off Linda by going out with Ruthie Lipson, a pretty girl from Cranston, Rhode Island. She lived in a six-room house with a broken picket fence and a small lawn of scorched, brown grass. She had long, scraggly, dirty-blond hair, a thin nose, ice blue eyes, and a large sensuous lower lip. Her favorite song was "Dim Dim the Lights" by Bill Haley and the Comets, even though it was, by that time, an old hit from 1954. She was always chewing Wrigley spearmint gum and reminding me that, unlike other girls I kissed, she didn't have halitosis. She had big tits and a small hard ass that felt like two cantaloupes.

The downside of Ruthie was that she wanted to dance every time we went out. I know you're thinking, "Wait, aren't you the founder of the Crazy Dance Club?" Yes, but I dreaded Arthur Murray-type ballroom dancing. I was self-conscious and couldn't move my feet without feeling like I was stepping into one bucket of liquid shit after another. No way was I ever going to Twist again like they did last summer. I did slow-dance with Linda in her basement. But when you're dancing slowly, no one can see that your feet don't know what they're doing. I would just as soon skip the dancing and hop with Ruthie into the red, plastic back seat of my black 1960 Dodge Dart convertible, which my parents had bought me as a graduation present.

I gave Ruthie the sterling silver ID bracelet Linda would never accept—only to take it back when Linda re-entered my life in the late summer. I know, I was a schmuck, but I'm sure Ruthie didn't want my goddamn bracelet after I'd broken up with her. I think she sensed it was kind of a summer fling.

That summer, I went to Cape Cod regularly with members of the Crazy Eight, who were crazier than ever. We stayed in Falmouth in a week-end rental. We often went to Hyannis Port for the day. Our senator, John F. Kennedy was campaigning for the presidency that year, and a large crowd was usually outside the gated entrance of the "Kennedy compound." The JFK groupies waited for hours to catch a glimpse of the royal Kennedys on their way in or out.

Like the Kennedy brothers (but less successfully), we were always looking for girls. We couldn't find many at the Cape, so one of the Crazy Eight suggested we all go down to the Newport Jazz Festival in Rhode Island.

Worcester and Providence, Rhode Island, were like bad brothers in a family of misfits with Boston as the cruel parent. They were connected by Route 146. We always seemed to be on that road—like ball bearings in a tilting glass tube—arguing, swearing, talking, smoking, drinking, and figuring out life, inaccurately. We arrived at the cobblestone streets of Newport. Having downed a few Buds on the way, I already had a buzz on and felt compelled to climb a large oak tree near the famed Newport Casino tennis club. I was hanging upside down from a bough when the rest of the Crazy Eight got into a brawl with some Rhode Island guys who'd been drinking hard. Jumping down from the tree, I came to the aid of the Eight.

Now we had a tagalong kid from Worcester named Barry Jagodnick. Barry had a distinct way of sauntering. His back always slanted in the direction from which he came, so he appeared to be simultaneously coming and going. Anyway, as I and the rest of the Worcester crew traded punches with these thugs, I yelled, "Hey Barry, get the cops! We're getting the shit beaten out of us!"

Barry looked at me as if I was crazy. Wiping blood from my mouth, I yelled again, "Get the fucking cops! These guys are going to kill us!"

While Barry sauntered off in search of law enforcement, we kept slugging. We ended up getting reamed, all Crazy Eight of us. We were lying on the side of the road, like flattened lizards, licking our wounds, when Barry finally returned, moving like a low-cruising, flying saucer.

"Barry," I gurgled, "did you get the cops?"

"Yes, I approached the policeman on the corner and told him."

"What the hell did you say to the cop?" I asked.

"I said, Officer, Officer, there is a fight pending."

I shook my head. "A 'fight pending?'" I repeated. "That's what you said? Did you tell the cop that we got the pending shit knocked out of us?"

The rest of that lazy summer saw more rumbles. We got into a big fight outside Providence's East Side Diner with a gang that hated anyone from Massachusetts. That was enough to get things started. There were lots of fights at Hot Dog Annie's, our hangout in Leicester, Massachusetts. Did Brewster prepare me for these battles? No, the City of Worcester did more than enough to steel me for the cruel world. Brewster was just a frightening detour with no redeeming value. I can't say I was schooled in all the right places.

CHAPTER 9:

College Days in Massachusetts

In September I set off to UMass-Amherst. This time my mother came along. I don't think she completely believed I'd graduated from high school and had been admitted to a college. All she ever wanted was for me to be a high school graduate and now she was about to get more. It was an event she had to touch and feel.

Amherst was only about an hour from Worcester. But I think my mother and I both hoped it would put some distance between us. It would relieve the tension. Maybe it meant I wouldn't come home on weekends, and she would have peace and quiet—which in reality, she didn't want. My father proudly drove our brand-new gray Peugeot. Just like I did when I was a small kid, I sat quietly in the back seat, looking out at the whizzing pine trees as we roared west up the Mass Pike.

I never wanted to arrive there. UMass was founded in 1863 as a land-grant agricultural college. Thousands of its students still came from farming towns like Paxton, Athol, and Greenfield. They were forking over $200 a semester to learn about fertilizer, feed, irrigation, and crop rotation. Agriculture? Hell, I didn't even rake the leaves at my house. Now I was about to be plopped into Old MacDonald's barn, filled with even more hayseeds than Wolfeboro, New Hampshire.

Amherst was also home to Amherst College, one of the elite "Little Ivies." Ivy is a creeping vine, invasive and destructive. David Halberstam's *The Best and the Brightest* explains how all the brains from Ivy League schools got us into Vietnam and fucked up this country's foreign policy.

Arriving on campus, we pulled up to Van Meter Hall, a sprawling red brick dormitory. I already knew who my roommate was going to be. The month before, my mother received a call from a Worcester lady who said her son, Donny Grant, was also going to UMass. Mrs. Grant thought Donny and I could bunk together. After meeting with Mrs. Grant, my mother sanctioned the union, even though Donny wasn't Jewish. The matchmaking seemed odd to me, especially since Donny didn't need any help making friends. He was the bright, rugged, handsome quarterback of North High's football team. He was famous in Worcester.

From the minute we met, Donny and I saw eye to eye on just about every subject. We discovered that our dorm had a lot of crazy freshmen from similar middle-class families. There were a lot of guys from around Boston, Brookline, and Newton who were as nuts as the Crazy Eight. Our first-floor, gray-cinder block, white-linoleum room became like the dorm's lounge. Everyone hung out there, smoking Lucky Strikes, asking Donny for homework help. He was not only a star athlete, but he also aced tests without ever seeming to study.

Donny was the intelligent one. I was the in-house color commentator, slinging sarcastic remarks about who at Van Meter was doing what to whom and when. As always, I told only original jokes. Almost immediately at Van Meter my popularity took hold like the night at Steve Burwick's. Best of all, none of those brutal assholes from my first year at Brewster showed up, much less on the UMass football team. Thank God.

That fall, JFK's election as president of the United States had implanted my latest ambition: after law school, I would become a U.S. senator from Massachusetts. For practice, I would first seek the office of president of Van Meter Hall. My opponent was a husky, round-shouldered, bear of a student known as "Big Mike" Steiner. He appeared highly electable in that most everyone considered him a large, hairy "nice guy." But I have always suspected that living inside every nice guy is a bad guy waiting to screw you over. The fact that everybody suddenly seemed to be named Mike also spurred me to run. I hated clichés. I lost by just a few votes. That was the end of my political career.

I did make the soccer team, as an alternate goalie. My only memory of being on the team is flying up in the air, my black-cleated shoes arched over my head, trying to stop a ball that was going into the net. I recall the ape-like coach—he had a shock of sandy blond hair that fell on his forehead like a traffic arrow—pulling me from the game. "The goddamn goal was your fault," he screamed. At least he played me.

* * *

In late fall, UMass' fraternities began seeking fresh meat—I mean, freshmen—to replenish their ranks. I knew that there were these weird clubs with Greek names that owned clapboard houses where guys partied off campus. They'd ask their "pledges," "You're not an asshole, are you?" If you answered, "No," then you could join a brotherhood of assholes.

Alpha Epsilon Pi (AEPi) had a coat of arms featuring a menorah, a lion, a fleur-de-lis, an oil lamp, a skull, and a diamond. The menorah tipped you that this was a Jewish frat. Its members gave me a tour of their frat house—showing me its kitchen full of roaches and dirty dishes, its unflushed toilets, and its messy bedrooms. You might ask why anyone would want to live in this dump. But when you're at an agricultural school, are you going to dig for turnips or join up with schmucks of your own kind?

One of the frat heads was Bobby Smith, a pasty guy from Newton who claimed he'd co-written the hit song "Shimmy, Shimmy, Ko-Ko-Bop," sung by Little Anthony and The Imperials. Whether or not Smith wrote it, I liked the "native dance" that went with it. So, I pledged to AEPi.

After getting my ass whacked until it was cherry red with the frat's polyurethane oak engraved pledge paddle, I joined nineteen other pledges for six weeks of servitude—making beds, washing dishes, scrubbing toilets, and any other humiliating chores the upperclassmen could think up. Enduring this scullery work did bring me closer to the other slaves. Mike Rubin's claim to fame was that he was a naturally blond, blue-eyed Jew. But he also had an innocence and curiosity that I grew fond of. He often told of his high school basketball coach, who suffered from rhotacization—the speech defect exhibited by "tweety wabbit" hunter Elmer Fudd. When Rubin tried out for the team, the coach told him, "Woobin, a wike you a wot. But a basketball pwayer you're not."

My two best pledge friends, Jack Benjamin and Lenny Castle, were hipsters from Newton. They both wore tapered black pants and pointed black shoes. Jack was a great dancer—the only guy who could Twist from one side of the room to the other without stopping. Lenny, who had greasy hair and a shovel jaw, was a larger version of Jack—equally irrational in a quieter way. They'd constantly be snapping their fingers. Apropos of nothing, Jack would stare at you and say, "You heard about it!" Heard about what? I never knew what he was talking about. If he said something incredible, as he often did, Jack would tell you: "Believe it, and if you can't, put a Believing Machine on your head."

As the pledges became closer, our older "brothers" would devise new hazing rituals to test our loyalty to AEPi. Once, the frat fiends rolled me around in fireplace ashes and poured hot chocolate syrup all over me.

Another night, they sent the pledges buck naked into the cold. We stood for hours in the snow until the fuckers finally let us back in.

Among the key perpetrators was frat president Barry Ravech. He talked through his nose, was a short, gratuitously mean guy who espoused the theory that if you let your hair grow out and gel it straight up, you would look taller. Excuse me, *be* taller. He'd walk around the frat house, yelling, "Men, grow taller!" Ravech would also superciliously instruct pledges, "If you want to be intelligent, associate with intelligent people and repeat what they say." But if he heard anyone utter anything clever, he'd jeer, "You *heard* someone else say that. That's not original!" When I left UMass I made a list of everyone who'd crossed me. It was a long index and Ravech made the top five.

Ranking right up there with him was our house manager, Bobby "Blockhead" Slesinger. He earned a special place in my spleen when he got between me and Linda. By this time, Linda had graduated from Classical and had started at Boston University. I felt her drifting away. Every day that I didn't call her I thought about her. You can imagine my excitement when, during one phone call, Linda said she really wanted to see me. She wanted me to visit her that weekend.

The Thursday before, I was in my statistics class, sitting with my close brothers, Jack and Lenny, in the highest tier of the auditorium. Statistics was a subject that gave me the same sort of cold sweats I'd experienced deciphering geometry. It was hard enough to focus on the standard deviation (a concept you will never use) but this day I couldn't hear a word the professor, Sargent Russell, was saying. That was because one of my fellow pledges had told me that "Blockhead" Slesinger wasn't going to let me see Linda, just to fuck with me.

Slesinger, who was sitting in front of me, turned and snidely said, "Golub, you're assigned to the House this weekend. You'll be washing floors and cleaning toilets."

"Oh, will I be doing that, Mr. Bobby?" I asked defiantly.

Rage ballooned inside my gray Champion sweatshirt as I thought about wringing out a wet mop instead of being deeply inside Linda's linen pants.

"Yes, you can forget your trip to Boston," he said, turning away, as though the matter was finished.

"Slesinger," I snapped, "I should punch you in the mouth."

He pointed to his cleft chin.

"Go ahead, Golub, hit me right here!"

That was all I needed to hear. I threw a right jab. It missed his chin but caught him square on his Jewish nose, which bled instantly.

He stood up, speechless. As blood trickled onto his red cardigan sweater, he began to weep like a chastised child.

From below Sargent Russell yelled, "What's going on up there in row 28? Is there some problem?"

"Things are fine, Professor," I called back. "Just a little argument."

Then Slesinger piped up. Clutching his bloody handkerchief, he whimpered, "Not very fine at all, sir! Golub here punched me! I have to go to the infirmary."

Then Slesinger sprinted out of the class.

"Mr. Golub, is that true?" Sargent Russell hollered.

"Yes," I replied.

Prof. Russell dismissed the class.

In Massachusetts, unlike a lot of other places in the world, whatever you do immediately comes back to haunt you. When the American colonists got rebellious, the British came after them. The state prided itself on being a bastion of discipline, honesty, and righteousness. It was more accurately characterized as home to the hooligan Red Sox fans and Italian and Irish mobsters.

About an hour later, I was suspended from the University of Massachusetts.

* * *

On the upside, I wouldn't have to do any fraternity house chores! I took the bus down the Mass Pike to Bean Town, thrilled to spend that sunny fall weekend in Boston with Linda.

I arrived at her dorm on Bay State Road. I sat on a sidewalk bench, nervously waiting for her descent to the lobby. She seemed to take hours. It was no different from when I waited for her at her home—with the exception that her brother wasn't there to call me an asshole, because he was at Brown University captaining the swim team. Finally, she emerged. I noticed she was wearing her charm bracelet, but my gold bulldog wasn't on it.

We went to a bar at Copley Square and sat near the window overlooking the MTA tracks. Everything in the place was painted matte black—allowing customers to scrawl white chalk messages. The walls were covered with graffiti and inane shit from other guys who'd been screwed over by Linda types. Public service announcements like: "Call Betty, 617-953-2390. She's a bitch but a good fuck."

I told Linda about my latest expulsion. She didn't share my look-on-the-bright-side view that it was a good thing because we got to see each other. The bar wasn't crowded, and that made things even more uncomfortable because there were no weirdos to point to that would make for conversation.

We got up to dance. Neil Sedaka's "Breaking Up Is Hard to Do," #7A on the jukebox, came on. Linda was wearing her starched white shirt with its upturned collar—the prim look that turned me on. But as our hips pressed against each other, she informed me she was having her period—or, as she put it, her "friend was visiting for a few days." I imagined a bright red person, like a local Indian with a headdress and moccasins, in the shape of a Tampax. When Chief Tampax was visiting, Linda wouldn't let me go down on her because she thought it smelled disgusting. When I was thirteen, some winos outside my father's store told me they didn't mind muff-diving because you had to be drunk to do it. But naturally, I was willing to try. When you're attracted to someone, you cannot help but eagerly lurch toward their genitals. When you deeply love someone, the odor magically dissolves into thin air. In those days women had forests of pubic hair and, if you were a Hells Angel, you earned "red wings" by going down on a woman when she was having her period.

Anyway, Linda's message was clear: She didn't want to go out that night, even though she had said she wanted to see me this weekend and I had gotten booted out of college to be there. The period was always a good excuse to get rid of a guy. That was our limited date. I departed with a heartache, a headache, and yet another case of blue balls. Linda was great at generating simultaneous medical conditions.

As I left Boston, I had that familiar peach pit in my stomach. There I was, driving down Route 9 once again without Linda in the passenger seat. Since I was banned from campus for a week, I had no choice but to return to my home with another scholastic boot print on my ass. As I walked up the blacktop driveway of 28 Wamsutta Avenue, I studied our small brick house, knowing my mother was inside dressed in her terry cloth bathrobe, toiling away in the kitchen, and that I was seconds away from her deadly, bloodcurdling screams. If only she would have sided with me now, I would've changed. But this time, she told me it was too late—I was on my own, a "grown man." My growing amount of body hair was evidence that she might be right. But, other than that caterpillar fuzz on my lip, I had a vivid sense of a never-ending childhood, destined to return again and again to my angry home ad infinitum.

* * *

After seven days, the university allowed me to return. My frat brothers didn't exactly welcome me back with open arms. A house meeting was called on Wednesday night. I was the only subject matter. As Greek dramas go, it wasn't as large or formal as the trial of Socrates, but my encounter with Slesinger generated much heated debate. Half of the room was literally screaming—in a Boston accent—for my blood while I sat being judged in the round. But then, one of the most influential frat brothers stepped forward. He gave an unexpected and heart-warming defense on my behalf—recalling how I'd grown up on the mean streets of Worcester, how I'd worked in my dad's grocery store, and how worthy I was of the Brotherhood. His Clarence Darrow moment came when, in summation, he asked, "Which one of *you* wouldn't have done the same as Golub if you hadn't been allowed to see your girlfriend?" That seemed to convince almost everyone—except Blockhead—that I wasn't such a bad guy. I was initiated about a week later. I was now a brother. From then on, Slesinger kept his distance from me.

* * *

In my sophomore year, my dream of being a star litigator like Robert Taylor in *Party Girl* surrendered to my ambition to get rich by joining the national money grab. Suppressing my theatrical urge, I declared myself a business major. My classes were held in Draper Hall—or, as we called it, "Draper High School"—an orange brick building with thin Ionic columns. Professor Rudolph Harold Kyler taught business administration, a course I never understood, mostly because I couldn't understand Kyler. He wore rumpled, oversized black suits and spoke with a heavy German accent. Confused yet dogmatic, he resembled the comedian "Professor" Irwin Corey. Kyler's name meant "little warrior" in German and no matter how many English words he butchered, he would bluster and stumble onward, riddling his teachings into an odd salad dressing of nonsense mixed with spoonerisms.

"You have to be careful of the people you meet on the road," he once told us. "When I was a young man, I met some very bad persons who had a terrible influence on me. You would say I got crooked up with mixed... Sorry, sorry! I mean mixed up with crooks."

And: "I was cooking dinner last night and I burned my hand, I mean my hand, and I should've used a hotch-polder, I mean a pot-holder."

He would use real-life rich people to make his points.

"If Nelson Rockefeller wants to buy 300 sports jackets, he can do it!" he'd say. "But pee weanuts cannot. ... I am so sorry. I meant, we peanuts cannot."

When it came time to hand out grades, you didn't find your score on the bulletin board. Instead, Kyler stood next to a stack of our exams and announced each person's grade—starting with the worst.

"Low honors go to Bob!" he'd blare. "Bob, you got low honors. You failed miserably! Get out of the class! And don't come back!" Kyler would then throw Bob's exam paper at him and point to the door.

"Second-low honors go to Jane," Kyler would continue. "That will cost you a plunty pretty, I mean a, a, a pretty penny. Now get out, Jane."

Halfway through the semester, most of the gray metal chairs in the class were empty. Even the students who'd hung on he'd call "stupid assholes going to university."

* * *

Between Prof. Kyler and "Blockhead" Slesinger, I was sick of UMass and wanted to transfer out. Naturally, I was thinking about a college in or near Boston. I still wanted to be closer to Linda, even after she used her cycle to pedal away from me. Little did I know how far away.

After my expulsion, when I returned to UMass, I called her from my dorm pay phone.

"Linda, I want to come to Boston this weekend," I began, my voice dropping, as it always did when I asked her out, as I always had to do. "Are you free?"

"I think I am busy," she answered in a soft, affirmative voice.

"Busy?" I said, emphasizing my mystification. "A friend of mine is having a great party in Cambridge."

I did have a new friend who did live in Cambridge and who did throw wild parties. But her silence told me that "friend," "wild," "Cambridge," and "party" added up to nothing. I wished I'd tried another approach. I knew I was not going to have a weekend with Linda, not even Friday night. I could tell by her goddamn "busy"-ness that the "busy" bitch was going to be seeing another guy.

Friends of mine had told me that she'd reconnected with an older guy from Worcester: Michael Gordon, a senior at the Massachusetts Institute of Technology. Gordon's father owned a wholesale meat company, Chicago Beef, where my father bought his sirloin, rib-eye, chuck, brisket, what have you. That put Michael Gordon in a superior position on the Worcester chessboard—certainly in the husband-hunting eyes of the Pauls.

Michael was the kind of guy who was initially friendly but, gradually, turned arrogant. He had a perpetual smile, shiny skin, a winter tan, and the air of unearned confidence. I'd heard about kids like him who polished their faces in the morning with special stuff. They would strut down the school corridors glistening like waxed fruit. They would use the mirror inside their locker to floss, as though they were getting ready to pose for a Tide ad.

I should have seen Michael Gordon coming. Linda had had her eye on him for years.

I remembered sitting with her on her Kensington Road stoop one afternoon. I was nineteen, she was eighteen. She was wearing loose-fitting, white, Bermuda shorts. I was telling her jokes that were making her laugh.

Her mother and brother weren't around. I thought maybe we were on the verge of going up to her pink bedroom.

Then out of nowhere I heard a siren. I thought it was the police, roaring up Kensington to arrest me for having fun with her. Instead, a fire engine-red Corvette pulled up and stopped at the curb. The noise was coming from the Corvette, and Michael Gordon was at the wheel. He turned down the siren.

"Hi Linda!" he called.

Seeing me, he added, "Hi Richard."

"Wanna go for a ride?" he said. "Ice cream?"

The Corvette had only two bucket seats. I couldn't believe that Linda—the wannabe Bohemian artist—would go for a guy who drove around blasting his siren like an old rabbi blowing the shofar. But obviously, I underestimated her love of fast cars and ice cream. After a moment of hesitation, she got into the car. I waited like a putz for her to come back. She returned from her joy ride with a large vanilla cone. Sprinkles decorated her hand. A walnut shard was lodged between her two front teeth. As Gordon vroomed down the hill, she asked if I wanted a lick.

It didn't occur to me until years later that she must have invited Gordon over knowing, full fucking well, that I was going to be sitting right there. She'd summoned both her suitors. Both wanted the same thing at the same time. And she loved it.

Now that we were in college, I knew she was taking birth control pills (which had been around for only two years) even though she was still "a virgin." She was screwing Gordon regularly, and me when necessary.

I gripped the black receiver of the dorm phone tightly as I struggled not to lose my temper. I should have done my impersonation of Brando in *The Wild One*: "You think you're too good for me? Nobody's too good for me! Anybody thinks they're too good for me, I make sure I knock 'em over sometime."

But, no, I just wimped out. I breezily told her it was "fine," and I'd call her soon. I let her sit on me like I was a rusted aluminum beach chair. I resigned myself to the picture of her gamboling out of her dorm in her starched white shirt and slipping into Michael Gordon's red Corvette.

CHAPTER 10:

Back to Worcester

In the fall of 1962, as I turned twenty, there was no way I was going back to state university. I was done with the country bumpkins of Western Mass. Instead, I began my junior year at Clark University—conveniently located in Worcester. Yes, that meant I'd be living at home again with the hysteria of my mother and my easygoing dad. My dad's stepbrother, Bill Brodie—my grandmother's second husband was named Brodie (from Brodinsky)—had attended Clark in the 1920s and he raved about it. I loved my Uncle Bill because he would talk to me about everything under the sun and, unlike Uncle Phil, my jewelry expert, he never played musical wardrobe. Uncle Bill wrote several books—like, *Keeping Your Church in the News*, which sold three copies.

Clark, founded in 1887, was a small university, two rungs below the Ivy League. It was famous for being the place where Sigmund Freud introduced psychoanalysis to America during five extemporaneous lectures in 1909. Freud came with his protégé, Carl Jung. As they steamed into New York Harbor, Freud reportedly told Jung, "They don't realize that we are bringing them the plague." If they were looking for disturbed Americans, they couldn't have picked a better place than Worcester. Its State Insane

Asylum had already been open for seventy-six years and even its "normal" citizens exhibited enough complexes to occupy Freud's couch for years.

Clark prided itself on being vaguely bohemian. A lot of bearded kids from New York City gravitated there—maybe because the school was famous for its liberal marijuana policy. It was one of the first schools to allow students to toke up anywhere, reinforcing the proposition that a university education was more about partying than learning.

I made it my business to get out of our house on Wamsutta Avenue as often as possible. During the week, I hung with the Crazy Eight in Worcester and, almost every weekend, I went to Boston. Linda and I were at different ends of Bean Town. I was informed that she and Michael Gordon spent most weekends rumbling up and down Beacon Street with shit-eating grins in his Corvette, top down, her curly, brunette hair blowing in the hard Boston breeze. When she wasn't upright in his sports car, I accurately imagined she was horizontal in his Cambridge flat.

But under no circumstances was I giving up without a fight. Each week I called her and tried to see her for coffee or a walk around the campus. We wrestled through countless conversations, face to face and on the dorm pay phone. The dialogue was always the same:

Me: "Do you still love me? Are you serious with this Gordon jerk?"

Linda: "Don't call him that! He's nice. You know I will always love you. I just like him. He's a nice guy. It's nothing serious."

I was like a loud housefly, well on my way to being swatted. But there was no way I wasn't going to hang in there. I couldn't get her out of my mind, and I knew the feeling was mutual. I was convinced that someday she'd be sorry and that gave me my minimum daily requirement of solace.

* * *

Meanwhile, I did my best to try to party her out of my mind. I looked about twelve but I had a high-quality fake ID that got me into all the dens of iniquity in the Combat Zone, as Boston's tenderloin was known. There was one strip club on Washington Street, Frankie's New Yorker, where I was treated with great respect. The bouncer, a large German guy named Fritz, always ushered me to the first row. I became friends with the strippers, who referred to me as "the kid." It was nice to be wanted someplace while I suffered through all the Linda shit.

In those days, most girls who weren't strippers viewed strip joints as dirty. When I'd invite a girl to join me at Frankie's, their knee-jerk reaction was, "How disgusting!" So, I was impressed when one of Linda's best friends, Deeny Yudell, accepted my invitation.

Like most of the pretty Jewish girls I knew, her father was a doctor and she lived in a ranch house with a picture window overlooking Worcester. Deeny had long wavy red hair, plump lips, and that sultry allure that made you scratch your crotch. Deeny liked me; I could sense it even though she was a little haughty and condescending. My motive in asking her out was twofold: (1) to make Linda jealous and (2), if the evening went well, switch Linda out for Deeny. That exchange move was in the back of my mind as we drove to Boston in my black Dodge. As she crossed her long shapely legs, I thought, "I could do this. I should do this!"

When we arrived at Frankie's, Deeny nonchalantly surveyed its décor. It has always fascinated me that women adjust so quickly to seedy circumstances. And, let me tell you, Frankie's was seedy, rank, and very dirty. I wouldn't elevate the description to funky. Its wall-to-wall carpet was saturated with piss and come. She should have freaked but she pretended to be above it all.

We settled into two well-worn leather seats in the front row. One of my favorite strippers, Ruby Red, came on stage, phantasmagorically dancing into a beam of ultraviolet light. She quickly snapped off her G-string. Her mossy muff was inches from Deeny's freckled face. Ruby's dry-humping did not faze my honored guest one bit. Rather, she watched the performance with rapt attention, almost like an OB/GYN student.

Trying to make conversation while I chugged a bottled Budweiser, I asked, "Can you imagine doing this for a living?"

"She's probably a hell of a lot happier than we are," Deeny quipped.

I'd met enough strippers by then to fully disagree with Deeny's statement. Strippers never seemed to be happy about anything. But what Deeny said had an undeniable effect on me. It brought me down. It made me worry that I would never achieve happiness. My mother used to warn me that, if I didn't get married, "You'll be living alone in one room in your sixties." I pictured myself as an old man, buying a blueberry crumb pie at 5 p.m., taking it home, and nibbling on a slice with a plastic fork while watching the local news.

I never went out with Deeny again. Maybe I saw her twice more on the street. (Whenever I see a friend, I usually calculate how many times I will see them in my lifetime.) It was a mistake not to see more of Deeny. Her remark stuck with me. It made me think she had the intellectual upper hand. She had a deeper view of humanity. We didn't belong together until I could be as happy as that stripper in Deeny's mind. I was either happy enough to go to Frankie's regularly, or I was unhappy enough to do so. I still haven't figured it out.

CHAPTER 11:

Meeting My Match

In 1962, I met a BU student named Alan Golden who offered me a way out of Worcester. Alan was from Woonsocket, Rhode Island. My naïve impression from all outward appearances was that his parents were New England rich. He stood about five-foot-eight, had straight platinum-blond hair, and did a very good Cary Grant accent. He chain-smoked, even as he handled the wheel of his black MG. By coincidence, I had recently convinced my parents to buy me an MG, albeit one that broke down most of the time. Alan had a cool third-floor apartment at 106 Myrtle Street on Beacon Hill. Just getting there—around a wicked curve with a blind spot—was a feat. But his parties were worth it. Almost every weekend, I'd find him holding a cigarette and a glass of white wine as he greeted guests at the front door.

Alan was always up for doing the wildest thing possible. In the summer of 1963, he and I got the brilliant idea to drive to Los Angeles, where I was due to attend UCLA summer school. Early in June, Alan's right and proper parents drove him between the white lines down to Worcester. After they bid him a safe trip, Alan and I loaded bottles of whiskey and an ice cooler into the new convertible that had replaced my undependable

MG. It was a black Dodge Dart with red leather seats. (I still don't know how my dad paid for it.)

After making a show of driving slowly and safely away from my house, we hit the gas and headed west. We took the southern route to LA. I had about as much connection to the South as my head had to my ass. But I soon found myself cruising down the dogwood-lined streets of Knoxville, Tennessee.

"Knoxvillian" was a demonym for a happy citizen who seemed to have walked straight off the set of *Ozzie and Harriet*. Inside their brightly lit houses, Knoxvillians sat down for home-cooked meals straight from the General Electric stove they'd picked out at Miller's Department Store. For a split-second I thought Linda and I could live in one of those white, clapboard houses, engulfed in azalea bushes which would protect us from the evil outside world. She could paint and I could be a country lawyer, like Atticus Finch in *To Kill a Mockingbird*. If only Linda would just calm the fuck down and break it off with Michael Gordon.

The next morning, we drove through Birmingham, Alabama. A speeding train nearly hit us as we crossed the railroad tracks. We never really paid attention to our surroundings—perhaps because we were drinking all the time. Birmingham looked depressingly industrial. That spring, Rev. Martin Luther King had organized his campaign for racial justice in Birmingham. At the time, we didn't appreciate the magnitude of that struggle. I did wonder what the hell two Hebes were doing in the heart of Dixie, Confederate flags flapping in the wind. My Dodge's Massachusetts plates were an advertisement for trouble.

Moving southwest across Mississippi, we drove day and night into the crepuscular beyond. We perfected a dangerous routine in which Alan and I would take turns driving—swapping seats while the car was moving. We did that once or twice a day, usually at 60 miles per hour.

We finally arrived in New Orleans. We found a flophouse where a withered bald reception clerk sat inside a nicotine-stained plexiglass box. Our room, up four flights, had peeling wallpaper, a putrid toilet, and a carpet that must have been a century old. Rather than taking a steamboat cruise or touring the French Quarter, we stayed entertained in our room by dropping water balloons on pedestrians. When we finally hit someone, the cops came up to question us. After listening to our vigorous denials for a half hour, they left—probably because they couldn't take the aroma of our bathroom.

Our first objective in New Orleans was to fulfill my childhood fantasy of bar-hopping down Bourbon Street—like every other sucker tourist. Right off the bat, we got into a row at one of those glaring neon clubs where we had to buy $40 shots before the "dancers" would talk to us. When we didn't buy a second shot, the bouncer tossed us onto the pavement. At least we heard Al Hirt play "Sugar Lips" before we got the heave-ho.

We spent just a day in New Orleans before moving on toward Texas. Alan made a good travel companion. He knew a lot of great jokes. None were original, but he had a real repertoire. He was always smiling, the right corner of his mouth turned up. I have always been fascinated by people who have what I call the "forever grin." They never completely close their mouths. You might wonder if they're thinking something underhanded or nefarious. But Alan just seemed to be enjoying life. I sometimes thought we were traveling across the states on that smile alone—that clever smirk seemed like a never-ending stretch of road.

* * *

It's always challenging to get into town at night. You need to formulate your objectives immediately, before you can see where you are. Where do we sleep? Where do we eat? Most importantly, where do we drink? Are there any girls around here? Is this a dangerous neighborhood? Where the fuck do we park the car without getting our shit stolen? Who would steal our worthless shit anyway? Maybe a homeless person.

One of the few things I knew about Houston was that its oil barons hung out at someplace called the Petroleum Club. I read about it in Life magazine. It was on the forty-third floor of the Humble Oil Building. Then as now, I saw the world as a chaotic place in a constant state of volcanic, vulgar upheaval. The Petroleum Club, like all clubs, was a means of avoiding or delaying chaos. It made its big-butted members feel ordered, stable, and normal.

We located the Humble Oil Building. Looking up from a parking lot across the street, I was sure those Texas wildcatters were up there, drinking exotic cocktails and dancing with beautiful women.

"Imagine those oil barons calling a company Humble," I said to Alan. "There isn't one ounce of humility in them! It pisses me off so much that you should sneak in with me."

Alan didn't answer me at first. Finally, he issued his diagnosis: "An inferiority complex is driving you to get into a place whose membership is founded on that complex. I don't have that problem."

It was quite an intellectual response from Mr. Party Animal. The reason he didn't have that "problem" was that he suffered from rich parents' syndrome.

Undeterred, I began to ponder how we might breach the forty-third floor. The only places I'd snuck into before were movie theaters and small high school football stadiums. As the red sun disappeared, the Humble Oil Building loomed. There was the real possibility of punishment. I hadn't thought about arrest since Bill Holloway and Dirty Art had invited me into their stolen car that dark day at Chandler Junior High.

Then I had a brainstorm. Alan would pretend to be blind. No one questions a blind person. I would be Alan's eyes. I would guide him right past security up to the Petroleum Club. I told him how simple it would be.

"Gol, this is crazy," he said. "I mean, *I'm* crazy and even I think it's crazy. Why the fuck do we have to do this?"

"Because there are beautiful women up there," I said, "and I want to meet them."

"That's not a good enough reason," he said.

"Because we are in this place," I explained. "This Houston place. And when you are in a place, you must act like you are in the place. If there is a club in that place, you try your ass off to get into it. Like Mount Everest. What does a mountaineer say when people ask why he climbed Everest? 'Because it is there.' That fucking Petroleum Club is there! We must make our ascent! Do you get it?"

Alan smiled, which I took for a yes. We had some passable clothes in our car. There in the parking lot, we changed into our finery—cuffed chino pants and wrinkled cotton sports jackets. We looked disgustingly preppy. It didn't occur to us that the security guard across the street might wonder why these two knuckleheads were using the trunk of a Dodge as a dressing room.

Alan clamped his eyelids closed, to appear blind. As an insurance policy, I put sunglasses on him. We ambled toward the Humble Oil Building. My hands were sweaty as I gripped Alan's arm tightly.

"Ouch," Alan yelped. "What the hell are you doing?"

"Well, then, grab *my* arm," I said. "Up to you."

He got into his role, leaning on me as I shepherded him, like a seeing-eye dog, through the glass door. To my amazement, the security guard didn't move from behind his desk. Instead, he smiled and politely asked for our membership number.

"Sorry," I answered quickly. "My dad's a member and I don't have his number."

Alan's fingers pressed into my arm.

"Tell him your last name is Aspray," he whispered. "Your father's name is Leonard."

Without hesitation, I muttered, "My dad is Len Aspray. This is my guest—Alan Lockstep."

"Fine," the guard said, "Just sign in and go on up."

I was instantly disappointed that I didn't hear a siren and hadn't gotten handcuffed. But Alan's upbringing had come in handy. I didn't know Aspray from hair spray. As I walked Alan over to an elevator, I asked, "Where the hell did you hear about Leonard Aspray?"

"I saw his name on the member list," he said.

The elevator opened into a lobby whose lighting was the color of honey. Sauntering in and out of the dining room were the oil barons and their matronly wives. Their daughters were authentic Southern belles—pampered debutantes who took WASPish allure way beyond what Worcester's girls had to offer.

Gazing out at the twinkling lights of Houston, I said, "Man, this is too good to be true! Let's have a drink."

"Good idea," said Alan. "Order me a Singapore Sling—easy on the gin and lots of grenadine."

Alan took his sunglasses off to drink in the view.

"Wow, Gol," he said. "You were right, this Petroleum Club is sensational. The glitz is fabulous." Alan was obsessed with the word "fabulous."

We sat down on two plush bar stools and ordered the kind of parasol-festooned cocktails we'd seen only in movies. Ray Charles sang "Take These Chains From My Heart" in the background. By the time our third drink came, the bartender was looking at us suspiciously. But the booze had only boosted our swagger. I scanned the packed dining room, where wine glasses clinked and elderly waiters laid crisp white linen napkins on members' laps. I wondered if we should ask the maître d' for a table by the windows and order dinner. The closest I had ever been to this scene was nervously listening to Linda talking about the Mount Pleasant Country Club, its tasty meals, extravagant desserts, and soaring dimpled golf balls.

"Gol, we should call our friends and tell them where we are," Alan said, imploring me with his wide-open eyes. "When are we going to get another chance like this?"

"First of all, shut your eyes and put on your fucking sunglasses," I whispered. "Where are we going to get a phone to use?"

Affecting an air of entitlement, I asked the bartender, "Sorry, I've forgotten—where's the telephone again?"

Without hesitation, he pointed toward the hallway. I grabbed Alan by the arm, and we walked over to a small, brightly lit room. A black rotary phone sat on a shelf, next to a sign that said, "WATS." I had read about AT&T's "Wide Area Telephone Service." The user paid a flat rate every month for unlimited use. My Worcester friend Abbie Hoffman used to sell a device called the Blue Box, which imitated dial tones, so you could make free calls from pay phones. It outsmarted "Ma Bell" (AT&T), a monstrous monopoly that abused its employees and customers. A WATS line was even more miraculous if you could get your hands on one. And you weren't really stealing, were you?

As soon as Alan and I saw that WATS line, we began calling our friends all over the country. Naturally, I rang Linda in her pink room.

"Just wanted to tell you we're in Houston," I said, thinking she'd be impressed that I was halfway across the country and had the beans to call her. "That's in Texas. We are headed to New Mexico tomorrow."

"That's nice," she said, as if she were speaking to a dry cleaner's delivery boy. She was no more impressed than if I were downstairs in her living room.

"We're at the Petroleum Club; surely you've heard of that!"

"Is that a gas station?"

As usual, she was bringing me down. I asked myself why I'd called her. Answer: because I had to. In fact, I wondered if I'd driven down here just so I could call her up there. If her lover boy, Gordon, was calling from Houston, she'd be howling "Remember the Alamo!" and asking him about his pickup truck.

"Have you ever been to Texas?" I asked, knowing she hadn't. I was ready to act shocked by this lapse in her sightseeing.

"Why would I go there?" she sniffed. "I'm not a cowgirl."

"And I am not a cowboy," I snapped, "but I am going west."

"I have to go," she said with the finality I had become accustomed to since the hayride.

"I already knew you had to go," I said. "I was just wondering when you would tell me that. And if you missed me."

I shouldn't have asked that last question, but I put it out there since I was halfway across the United States. My long way to sojourn might produce a "yes."

"You know how I feel about you," she purred.

In the annals of bullshit that wasn't an answer; it was another spin on her Limbo-rama.

"Of course, I do," I said. Pushing the envelope right to the glue, I added, "You're madly in love with me. Do I have to say it?"

Throughout the call, Alan was mouthing, "Tell her to fuck herself, Gol! Tell her now! Do it!" He was so prescient in that golden moment that should've been the turning point, the moment to terminate the retroactive torture she inflicted starting from the moment I jumped into that wagon straw. End it right now—stop the bleeding right there in the Petroleum Club. I didn't have the guts.

154

The phone went dead. Was I ever going to get through to her, or would I have to go down a manhole, squirm like a slug through the plumbing system of the Mount Pleasant Country Club, burrow up and out of a toilet in the clubhouse to get to her on the driving range?

Alan and I must have spent an hour in the phone room, laughing and boasting to our friends about the Petroleum Club. Suddenly, there was a polite knock on the door. Two large men in black suits were standing outside.

"We'll be out in a minute," I said with a smile. "Just wrapping up a call."

"Gentlemen, come out now!" ordered one of the men.

Bracing myself for some tough questions, I opened the door.

"What's your name, boy?" asked the larger of the two bouncers. "How'd you get in here? You ain't no member."

Continuing with our line of bullshit, I said, "My father is Leonard Aspray and he's a member."

"Leonard Aspray died five years ago," the bouncer informed me.

"So what?" I snapped. "I didn't say he was alive. I just said he's my father."

"Well, to my knowledge, he didn't have any kids," he snarled. "You'll have to leave the club unless you can show me identification that says 'Aspray,' or prove you're his kid and you still have a membership."

Alan was holding onto my arm like he was Helen Keller, but the guard noticed something missing.

"What happened to your sunglasses?" he asked.

I instantly wished we could get back to the bar where we'd once been safe with our cocktails. Things started to go blurry. I saw only one thing—the black-and-white wallpaper covered with a pattern that resembled a Rorschach test.

"Ink blots!" I blurted out. "Ink blots! Can't you see the ink blots?"

Sounding completely nuts, I pointed at the wall and ceiling. The bouncers stepped back to look for the ink blots as I pulled Alan away quickly, asking myself how they could be interested in the ink blots. Alan and I backed toward the elevator, whose door fortuitously slid open at that moment. We were out of there.

Back in the car, Alan became quite sick. He got out of the front seat and, resting one hand on the front fender, he leaned over and chucked up everything he'd consumed at the club. I couldn't help laughing. That's always my reaction when someone throws up. I laugh—and then I start to puke. Like clockwork, I vomited on the other side of the car. Perhaps I'd had a few too many at my new favorite oil club. But Alan was in far worse shape. His face was flushed, and he had a wicked fever. We'd been hoping to drive to New Mexico but, at 11 p.m., we decided to spend the night in Houston.

In the distance was a flickering neon sign that read, **LAS VEG S MOT R INN**. We were not going to hold the missing letters against them, so we drove over. The motel was lit up and jumping. "Short-stay" customers were pulling in and out. I never understood why my mother would blow a gasket every time I used the word "motel"—until one day she explained, "A motel is a place where men go to screw whores." We didn't have any intention of screwing whores—although that would've been a terrific outcome—but we did need a room. Looking back, I don't know why we didn't just sleep in the car. But two college kids apparently found it necessary to have conventional lodging.

Not that we were willing to pay for it. Our usual MO was to wait until someone was checking out and then take over the room, because guests tend to leave the room unlocked when their stay is over. The other option was to check the doors to the rooms in the hope that one would be unlocked.

That night, Alan was getting sicker by the minute; he must have had a 103-degree fever. He was sweating like pot roast. I was worried about him and feeling tired myself. So, we wasted no time letting ourselves into an unlocked room on the second floor. The only problem was that, based on the suitcases inside, it was still occupied. We didn't give a shit. We figured we'd sleep for a couple of hours and maybe the occupants wouldn't return until much later.

About two hours later, the door opened. Groggily, I saw two adults and two children backlit in the doorway of the room. They turned on the lights and saw us sprawled in our underwear on their beds.

One of the kids asked, "Mommy, who are these naked men?"

The mother screamed out something ungodly. We scrambled, grabbing our clothes and running past them.

We were in the Dodge racing through the night, well outside of Houston, when it occurred to me to check our crumpled road map. Everyone in my family has a terrible sense of direction. Once, when I was about ten, we were in Washington, D.C., trying to find a distant cousin, Leon Zygier, a nice man with a hunchback, who owned an appliance repair shop in the boondocks. My dad asked an old Black gentleman for directions. The man drawled, "Go to Ken Tuck Ave., but first follow R-rah Street." Or so my dad thought. We spent the whole sweltering day driving in circles before it dawned on me that the old man had really said "Kentucky Avenue" and "R Street." My dad kept telling me, politely, to keep quiet.

Now I was lost as shit in Texas. My compadre was out cold, snoring away, dripping sweat on the red leatherette back seat. I thought that we were driving west because I saw a sign that had a "W" on it. But who really knew? It was around 2 a.m. There wasn't another car on that pitch-black two-lane road. "I'm not going to turn around," I kept telling myself. "I'm not going to quit." I was getting a migraine headache.

I pulled onto the shoulder to piss. Maybe some fresh air would help. I stepped out of the car, away from Alan's moribund groans. As I pissed in the darkness, I heard a cacophony of crashing, hammering, and clanging. I saw a jumble of scissoring steely dinosaurs moving up and down around me. It scared the shit out of me. Judging by the noise, they were moving in my direction, ready to cut me in half with their claws. I jumped back into the car. Hours later, I realized they were oil rigs, pumping greasy dollars, giving meaning to the expression "making money while you're sleeping."

I kept driving until I couldn't hold up my head. Around 4 a.m., as we entered the town of Sealy, a mirage-like red and green neon sign announced the Stephen F. Austin Motel, named after the "Father of Texas." I pulled into the parking lot just as a man in an RV was pulling out. He rolled his window down and said, "This is a great place to stay. Do you want our room? We're leaving early."

"Sure! Which one is it?"

"Straight back—number 106. The door is open."

This was a godsend. I felt that our luck was changing. I parked the Dodge and pulled Alan out of the car. Bedsheets were piled up on the floor, but I felt grateful to have a bed. Minutes later, we were both fast asleep.

Around 7 a.m., I heard a knock on the door.

Hey, you with the Massachusetts plates," said someone with a Texan twang, "please stop by the office to pay your room charges."

I shook Alan awake.

"Someone's out there and they want us to pay for this room," I said. "Let's get the fuck out of here!"

I wasn't the least bit tired now. Alan seemed to be feeling better and chuffed up for a fresh challenge.

"You walk toward the office, acting like you're going inside to pay," I said. "I'll drive slowly, put the top down, and then you jump in."

Our sleep-and-split plan had gone perfectly. When I pulled alongside Alan, he leapt into the back seat and soon we were off down Route 90 West, the rising sun at our backs.

"Damn that was fun," I said. "Three hours of sleep and we're back on the road."

Alan climbed over the passenger seat, joining me in the front, as we passed a Kingdom Hall of Jehovah's Witnesses church. We'd been cruising for about 10 minutes when I noticed a green Lincoln Capri coming on fast in my rearview mirror. What the f was that about? I goosed the Dodge up to around 90 mph, but the Lincoln was now out of my mirror and thundering alongside us.

Glaring at us were two shit-kicking Texans with broken-in gray Stetsons and the steely gaze of Lyndon B. Johnson.

"You didn't pay for that room!" the guy on the passenger side yelled over the wind and dust. "Pull over, you assholes!"

The Lincoln's whitewalled Firestone tires inched in front of ours, nudging us off the road, onto a hot, rocky, cactus-lined shoulder. I pumped the brakes until the Dodge stopped.

A tough-looking dude in a lemon-yellow Western shirt and black boots jumped out of the Lincoln. He moved like a bullet toward me. Judging by the fire in his eyes, he was ready to brand my ass with a cattle iron—because the good Lord had told him to do so. But before he could put his hand on my door handle, I "scrubbed out," as we say in Worcester, leaving a cloud of dirt, dust, and gravel. I gunned the Dodge to 95 MPH and smugly said to Alan, "Look for the map. Let's get off this road and ditch them."

Alan rifled through the glove compartment, reporting its contents: "An empty bottle of rye…some broken pencils…a drained dry can of

Budweiser." Finally, he produced a frayed Texaco road map. He stared at the map while I drove straight ahead, sure as a baseball going over the fence that it was going to be a home run.

"Where do we go from here?" I asked.

"Go?" he said, squinting at the wind-whipped map. "There is no place to go. This is it!"

"It?" I asked.

"It!"

"It?

"Route 10 is it. There ain't no other it. My way or the highway and we are on the highway."

I began to understand why those two Texans didn't continue the chase. Their Lincoln could have outrun our Dodge; it had a V-8 engine, with much more horsepower than my six cylinders.

I looked down the blacktop that ran straight into the horizon. Shimmering in the distance were five large figures standing in the middle of the highway. As we drew closer, I could make out their tan pants and white shirts, their pointy boots, their Western hats, and their five-point star badges. Three Texas Rangers highway cars were parked across the road—fortified by a wooden barricade and a large red STOP sign.

Alan sized up what awaited us and screamed, "Another fucking cliché to tell my parents about! Stopped at a roadblock and arrested by Texas Rangers—key to the cell thrown away."

He looked at me for redemption, as if I could make this all go away.

When we finally arrived at our fate, I pulled to a stop. The largest Ranger walked to my side. He looked in the back seat and over at Alan, who sat frozen, staring straight ahead with his hands folded.

"You boys know about the Stephen Austin Motel up the road?" he asked, wiping his lips with the back of his hand.

"Yes sir, I do," I answered.

I wasn't about to lie under these barren circumstances. There wasn't another car or human around; it was just us and the law.

"Friend, please get out of the car," he instructed. "Place your hands on the car door."

I obeyed. I must admit these Texas Rangers were not as ornery as the ones I'd seen on the TV series *Tales of the Texas Rangers*. Marching band horns and drums from "The eyes of Texas are upon you," echoed over and over in my head as were about to be hauled off to a Lone Star jail.

After conferring with his colleagues, the big Ranger said, "Friend, kindly get back in the car and drive back to the Stephen F. Austin Motel. We'll talk there."

We were not about to mess with these cops. As soon as I turned the Dodge around, I said to Alan, "Whatever money we have left …"

"You mean $150 and change?" he asked. In those days, change was meaningful.

"Yes, take all of it and hide it in the air vent below the dash."

Alan stuffed the small wad into the vent. Under no circumstances did we intend to pay for Room 106.

"What the fuck am I going to tell my parents?" I wondered aloud. "That I have been arrested by Texas Rangers? Shit, that would get me on the front page of the *Worcester Telegram*."

We drove back slowly, followed by a caravan of flashing patrol cars. At the motel, we parked alongside the office. It felt like being outside Rader's office at Worcester Academy on the day they gave me the boot. The lead Ranger told me to talk with the manager.

Inside the hot motel office, I recognized the manager as the passenger in the Lincoln.

"This here office is not air-conditioned," he grinned, "as you may have noticed, there aren't many trees in Texas. We don't believe in much shade. Personally, I like a nice long drought."

Finally, he got to his point.

"That there room you were in is a good one with a double bed. It costs $18 a night. Which one of you is gonna pay for that night of shut-eye?"

"We only have about $5 that we saved for gas," Alan said meekly. "Didn't that family with the motor home pay for the room? The people who left around 5 a.m.?"

"That was their room, not yours," snarled the manager. "That dog isn't wagging its tail now. You slept there and you gotta pay."

This ugly banter went on for most of the morning as we sat in that oven—us insisting we had no money, the Ranger, who'd joined us, threatening to put us in jail.

"I can give you a check," I offered. "I have a checkbook in the car."

"I am not going to take a damn check from some Yankee fucking kid," the manager blurted.

The Ranger pulled the manager outside. They were gone for about thirty minutes.

When they returned, the manager said, "All right, but this check better be good."

"It's good," I said. "I have over $50 in my account at Commerce Bank in Worcester, Massachusetts." As if Commerce Bank meant something out here in cowboy hell.

I handed the manager a check and we hit the road. I later called Commerce Bank to put a stop-payment on the check.

* * *

We didn't spend much time in Austin, pressing on to El Paso, then crossing the Paso del Norte International Bridge into Juarez, Mexico.

We had never seen anyplace like it in America. Under the bridge, along the garbage-strewn banks of the Rio Grande, scores of shoeless peasant kids hollered for money—holding up long wooden poles with buckets in the hope that *turistas* would toss American coins over the railing. I can still hear them in my sleep, though I don't get out of bed to donate.

"*Señor, por favor,*" each of them pleaded. "*Dinero, dinero, por favor.*" They were not unlike Wall Street financiers I'd meet later.

Despite the intense heat, the men wore wool blankets called *serapes.* They tended to be shorter than Americans—humble and soft-spoken. Many seemed afraid to look me in the eye.

We walked around Juarez's unpaved streets. As we tried on sombreros, we were surrounded by blind beggars, beggars with infants, beggars with leprosy, beggars with no limbs. Kids, sometimes accompanied by skeletal dogs, asked us if we wanted to see the churches and other *puntos* of interest. That question was often followed by, "Do you want to fuck my sister?" Or "Do you want to fuck my mother?"

Alan replied, "Fuck your sister? *Señor,* I wouldn't even drink the water here." It was an old joke but we were in the middle of it.

There were more strip joints than one could count but most were too disgusting to hang in—full of drunken hombres with upside-down smiles who were not afraid to give a gringo a punch in the gut. There were no female patrons, aside from barflies trying to stand up in beat-up high heels and ripped stockings.

Prostitution was legal in Mexico, so thousands of American kids like us were cruising border towns and Mexicans were eager to take them on a vice ride. Together, with Tecate and margaritas, sex fueled the country's economy. There were so many brothels in Juarez, the whores should have had their own Yellow Pages. Someone in the street was constantly asking if we wanted to see a woman sit on a Coca-Cola bottle. Or a Donkey Show, where a woman and a donkey had sex. But that was too much even for us.

We soldiered on, determined to find a whorehouse come hell or high water. A street vendor told us about one that was a short cab ride away. I'd been to a brothel only once before, and it hadn't gone well. Two of the Crazy Eight and I had driven to the Bronx, where I was set up with a girl who had a tattoo above her shaved pussy that read "JAE." She was way ahead of her time. I asked her whose initials they were, prompting her price to shoot up from $5 to $25. When I refused to pay, the brothel's superintendent chased us down the steps and around the corner. Notwithstanding that experience, I figured that a whorehouse was safer than hooking up with a girl on the mean streets of Juarez.

So, we took a taxi to a part of town filled with churches, funeral parlors, and cathouses. Our destination was a pink, one-story adobe building with a sign that said San Souci (fancy French for "without worry"). We pushed open an old wooden door that hung from one rusted hinge. The door dragged loudly across the cobblestones as we stepped into a foyer reminiscent of a hospital's circular triage. There we beheld the owner of this fine establishment—a scabby, bowlegged, sunbaked madam who must have been in her seventies. She wore a gauzy cotton dress and scuffed white high heels. She met Alan with a dripping wet cheek kiss. I avoided my turn.

"*Señores, buenos dias!*" she said, whistling the words through the wooden pegs that served as her teeth. "You want to see the girls? We have the prettiest senoritas in Mexico, *muy linda*! You can fuck them! *Venga aqui?*"

She guided us into another large circular room, where the girls sat or stood along the wall, each gawking at us and probably thinking, "Shit, I have to fuck another stupid college gringo." There were no other patrons, probably because it was siesta. We next met Carlos, the madame's plump superintendent (every Spanish brothel has one). Carlos waddled across the room and extended one of his filthy hands to shake ours.

"*Señores*, you would like to choose one of the girls?"

He acted as though time was of the essence—as though there would soon be no girls left in Mexico. Most of these "girls" were old, obese, or homely. Alan, who didn't seem like he wanted to be there, selected a short, slatternly woman I wouldn't have fucked with his dick. Then, out of the pack, appeared a brunette, about twenty years old, pretty in a Natalie Wood way. She wore a bright red dress and a hard expression that barely concealed her annoyance. In other words, she was my type.

Introducing myself as "Frank," I took her by the hand, which she limply gave me. I was excited and raring to get it going. The super escorted us into a warren of shabbily built rooms, insulated from each other only by wood framing and diaphanous fabric. Privacy was just a figment of the imagination. You could see into the next so-called room.

Once we were in the room, I took off my Levi's and let this Natalie of Juarez touch my *verga,* which was rock hard.

"*Quiero ocho?*" she asked, meaning she wanted $8.

"I will give you seven," I countered.

"*Ocho.*"

"Seven."

This went on for much too long. I wasn't going to pay eight and she wasn't going to accept seven.

"Okay," I said. "I'll give you eight for a blow job *and* you have to fuck me."

Once she agreed, a gaunt, gray-haired Caucasian woman entered the room. She wore a white uniform and carried a roll of toilet paper.

"*Señor*, I am the nurse," she said in English worthy of a Wellesley grad. "I am here to examine you for venereal disease."

Before I spoke a word, her clammy hand was examining my *verga*, rolling it back and forth like a cigar being made.

"You appear clean," she said. "Do you have syphilis or gonorrhea?"

"No, I do not," I answered promptly, eager to get to the main event before this nurse completely degraded my almost-hard-on.

"*Bueno, señor,*" she said. She turned to visit Alan, whom I could hear talking to his afternoon date, sounding almost like he was trying to stall.

I laid down on the bed, which was more like a raised floorboard. Natalie reluctantly went to work—allowing only about a centimeter of my dick into her mouth, about as far as her clenched teeth. There was no way my little battering ram was going to bring down that enamel door. She reminded me of a Worcester girl who once twisted my dick into a pretzel, believing that gave me pleasure.

I finally told her to stop, figuring that I would move to the second course on the menu. I had a condom. There was no way I would screw her without one, and I wanted to tell everyone back home that I had fucked a whore in Mexico. (A girl once said to me, "Stop trying to fuck me. You don't want to do it; you just want to tell your friends about it.")

I began to lower her shoulders toward the mattress, but she vigorously resisted.

"*Paga!*" she commanded. "*Paga, ahora!*"

Her angry expression told me she wanted to be paid.

It didn't take long for the madame and the super to barge into the room. They must have been standing in the corridor. Surrounded, I was escorted to the big circular room, where the whores curiously smelled like limes. Alan soon appeared. He was fully dressed, still bargaining with his choice the whole time.

"I thought you said five," he told her. "I am willing to give you four."

He stood behind me, laughing, possibly enjoying the negotiation more than the experience. In the meantime, I was in a serious conversation with that lovely couple, the Madame and the Super.

"Look here," I said, "she agreed she would blow me, then fuck me for $8. I only got this terrible, seriously bad, blow job. No *bueno!* Now she doesn't want to fuck me. I want half my money back!"

While the words were tumbling out of my mouth, I understood how farcical the situation was. I was complaining about a defective service— like complaining to the manager of a car wash my tires weren't scrubbed.

"We give you nothing more," the madame advised. "You got sucked and that is all, señor. Just suck! Now *vamanos!*"

We paid up. But, walking out that front door into the late afternoon sun without a sombrero, I couldn't let it go. I knew that I had been cheated. A blow job is not a fuck, especially after we'd come all the way from Worcester, Massachusetts. I spotted an older, melon-faced policeman in a dark blue uniform. He seemed approachable, so we registered a complaint.

"Excuse me, officer," Alan said, "We were just inside the brothel over there and my friend was promised something that he didn't get. Can you help us?"

"I didn't get to have sex," I eagerly interjected. "You know… I didn't fuck one of the girls."

"No, *señor*," the officer replied, "you have to go to the *Federale Policia*. I am just a Juarez policeman, local."

He pointed down the street to a white adobe building with bars on the windows.

The jurisdiction issue wasn't clear to me. I was also struck by the proximity of the brothel and the police station—whores and cops, side by side, like horseradish applied to herring. It crossed my mind that we were spending *mucho* time with cops, in two countries, and that it probably wasn't healthy. But this time we were representing the sex life of red-blooded American guys, which doesn't last that long.

Stepping into the station, we spied two cells containing four savage-faced prisoners, grumbling in Spanish and smelling of *cerveza* and *mierda*. One of them kept thrusting his calloused fingers, tattooed "love" and "hate," toward me through the bars, grabbing at the space he could not inhabit. An overhead fan, seemingly made of black leather, stopped and started as if a kid were flipping the switch. Near a tipsy three-legged table stood a stocky policeman in a rumpled khaki cap.

"Sir," I announced, "I would like to report an incident."

"*Si, hombres, que pasa?*" he inquired.

"A few minutes ago, we were at the place, the whorehouse, called Sans Souci," I recounted. "I paid for a blow job—plus I was supposed to fuck the same whore, too. She only gave me a blow job. I want one half of my money back. I paid $8!"

The sum of money sounded awfully small. Maybe I should have said $10, but Golubs don't lie.

Alan took this opportunity to ask, with his usual shit-eating grin, "How *was* the blow job? Was it worth it?"

I didn't reply, wanting the cop to take my complaint seriously. It was my firm legal position that not getting to fuck a prostitute was a serious breach of contract in Mexico, where prostitution was a major industry.

"Your *pasaportes*," he requested. "*Por favor.*"

No one told me you needed a passport to screw a hooker.

"Passports?" I replied. "We don't have any. We came in on our drivers' licenses."

"*Bueno, señor,*" he said. He examined our Massachusetts and Rhode Island licenses as if he understood the details and then politely handed them back to us.

"*Venga,*" he said, beckoning us to follow him into the street. Before leaving, he pointed to a large portrait on the wall, proudly saying, "*El presidente!* Adolfo Lopez Mateos." I guess this was meant to demonstrate that Mexico had a real government and laws, or that the president had been to the same brothel.

The three of us marched to the funk-ridden doorstep of the Sans Souci, where the officer approached the madame.

"These Americanos, one of them, claims that he wasn't given what he paid for," he said. He pointed to me, adding, "He says he was supposed to have *sexo*, but he got no *sexo* and he paid $8."

I was beginning to understand that I wasn't the first complainant to return to the Sans Souci. The madame offered a one-dollar refund and a discount on my next visit.

"No," I protested. "I want one half of my money back!"

It was a genuine Mexican standoff. I was certain that sticking to my guns was a smart negotiating strategy, even when dealing with a whoremonger.

The madame handed me eight wrinkled dollars.

"You have your money back," she smiled. Then, flashing those pegged teeth and pinching her small boobs, she added, "*Señor,* you come back here after midnight, and I will give you a free fuck."

"Don't wait up for me," I replied.

* * *

We gratefully headed back across the border, driving around the clock as usual, sharing the grueling nighttime straightaways. About 5 a.m., Alan was driving and intermittently falling asleep at the wheel. Both of us were in desperate need of sleep, so we pulled over at a dilapidated concrete building whose putrid, green swimming pool and crippled VACANCY sign hinted that it might once have been a motel. Its office lights were off. We were about to get back into the car when a short-haired, consumptive-looking person emerged from behind the building.

"You lookin' to get some shut-eye?" he growled. "How many are you?"

Plainly, there was no one else, but this wasn't the time to be a wise-ass.

"Just the two of us," I answered.

"Follow me," he cried out as if we were going into battle.

He led us into the misty desert as the sun rose. We hiked for a mile through cacti, coyotes, and sagebrush. I began to wonder if this grizzled motelier might be a serial killer, ready to bury us among the prairie dogs and Gila monsters. Finally, we arrived at a weathered Quonset hut. It looked like the fuselage of a plane that had crashed. Or maybe the last home of a down-and-out family that had moved on decades ago.

The motel manager unlocked the front-door hasp. We nervously entered this dented tin can, filled to the brim with darkness and the miasma of piss.

"Wait a second," the manager exclaimed. "Let me light this place up!"

A flickering bulb hanging from a frayed cord revealed a floor of sand and rock and one piece of furniture—a Procrustean campaign bed made of rusted springs and splintered wood.

"What's that?" I asked.

"It's a nice bed," he answered, as if he were showing off a room at the Ritz.

"Really?" Alan deadpanned. No one could say "really" as archly as Alan. He owned that word.

"How much do you want?" I groaned. "It's nearly 6 a.m."

"Six dollars and you gotta git by 10 a.m.," he barked, as if he had the last available suite for a king's coronation and another sucker was arriving any minute.

"We'll give you four," I said. "That's all we got and it's only four hours."

"I wouldn't rent this room here to Jesus Christ for four dollars!" said the host.

There was silence—no give from either side. Our Conrad Hilton shut off the light and locked up his corrugated hut. The three of us trudged back across the desert silently.

Somehow daylight and the morning air revived us. We got back behind the wheel of my Dodge, bound for the Grand Canyon. We arrived at its South Rim around 9 a.m. The touted wonder of the world was ringed with camping vehicles. Determined to have a clear view, we found a point where we could peer a mile down. Into this void we began throwing paper airplanes—watching them spiral and soar, one after the other, on their missions.

The canyon was so deep that we couldn't see where most of the planes landed. But I spotted about a dozen lying on a ledge below. Since we'd run out of paper, I figured we should fly them again.

"I am not going down there," Alan made clear. "You have to be crazy …"

"On my way," I said as I slid over the railing.

I started to climb down the side of the canyon. A few minutes later, I stood thirty feet below on a small cliff about six feet wide. I began to launch the paper airplanes I found among the scrubs. Above me, Alan was loving it.

After my squadron had flown, I idiotically moved closer to the edge and craned my neck trying to see the bottom of the canyon. Hot blood shot up my legs into my pelvis. "We love precipices," the actor Richard Burton once said. "We look to go to the edge and withdraw. Sometimes we go over." In those days, I had no fear of heights, but now I was teetering on a rock sill that must have been ten skyscrapers high. I began to wonder if I'd ever watch another Yankees-Red Sox game. All because of some fucking paper airplanes.

I turned my back to the canyon and started climbing up its 90-degree vertical wall. My Converse sneakers searched for solid rocks. I gripped whatever handhold I could find—until there weren't any left. Alan was still fifteen feet above.

I spied one scrawny dwarf pine growing out of the rock face and lunged for it.

Alan shouted, "Gol, stay right there! I'm going to call the rescue squad!"

He sounded more frightened than I was. And by then I was numb with fear.

Clinging to the pine, I asked, "How the hell do you know there *is* a rescue squad?"

"Gol, I just assumed there was a rescue squad. This is a good place for one, don't you think? The fucking Grand Canyon?"

Mosquitoes swarmed around my face. I didn't have one available limb to swat them.

The pine began to crack. I could see it pulling free from the rock. Pebbles tumbled downward.

Hoping the pine would last, I used it to stretch higher. I found more crevices. I used them to pull myself up, little by little, until I saw Alan's outstretched hand. He pulled me to safety.

"Gol, you're such an asshole!" he screamed, shaking his head. "You are! You are a crazy asshole! Welcome back to the real world."

CHAPTER 12:

Vegas is Not for Kids

Back in the car, we headed for the Hoover Dam. We took a long walk around it, looking down on Lake Mead—this time, staying behind the guardrail—and touring the dam's generators.

But all that was really in our heads was the city in the desert, Las Vegas. I kept saying to myself, "If you build it, they will come!" I don't know why I said that. It must have been related to Bugsy Siegel building The Flamingo casino. In any case, we were coming!

Our Dodge was soon rolling up the long driveway of The Sands Hotel and Casino. Its marquee—with an S five times the size of the other letters—advertised Red Skelton, one of the silliest men who ever lived and who never learned to speak any known language.

We chose The Sands—"A Place in the Sun," the marquee said—using the same technique that had served us well at Houston's Petroleum Club. Alan had read, in a Rhode Island newspaper, that a high roller—last named Lerner—had recently been gambling at The Sands as a VIP guest of the resort's general manager, Jack Entratter. We decided that Alan would pose as Mr. Lerner's cousin, in the hope that Entratter would give us similar VIP treatment (including a free suite). Entratter was known as "Mr.

Entertainment"—even though he himself didn't smoke, drink, or gamble. He had managed the famed Copacabana nightclub in New York. He was tight with Frank Sinatra, who'd gotten married to Mia Farrow at Entratter's apartment. Sinatra, and his Rat Pack, had shot *Ocean's Eleven* at The Sands, and Entratter had built them a special club there called the Copa Room.

What we didn't know was that Entratter reported to mob bosses Meyer Lansky, Doc Stacher, and Hyman Abrams, who controlled The Sands. We didn't have a clue who we were fucking around with when we strolled up to the reception desk and asked to see Jack Entratter. Out came a hulking man—he'd been a bouncer at The Stork Club—whose slicked-back, white-sidewalls hair had a left-side part as precise as a racetrack. He smiled and flashed his black bottomless eyes. He was rough around the edges but, I have to say, he was quite nice to us, especially considering we were bullshitting him. He complimented Lerner over and over—remarking what a gentleman Lerner was and how much he enjoyed his stay at The Sands. I pictured Lerner walking around the casino, saying out loud, "I am really enjoying my stay!"

Evidently, Lerner left the week before. It was a good thing we arrived when we did. For all we knew, Lerner was a gangster. But Alan didn't give a shit. He laughed uncontrollably to himself as we signed the registration. We were hoping Entratter would "comp" us but at least we got a "rate," a 50 percent discount. It had all been so easy—except that I was hoping and praying Entratter wouldn't call Lerner, who was probably in his office in Woonsocket with his legs up, drinking a Maxwell House decaf and free as a bird to answer his phone and say, "Who da fuck is Alan Golden?"

A blue-and-gold-clad bellhop, whom we conveniently forgot to tip, delivered us to our room.

"Gol, we did it," Alan yelled. "Jeez, just look at this fucking room and we are paying almost nothing for it."

The room was crème-colored with heavy, red-trimmed, white drapes, and old Hollywood furniture—two white, barrel-studded chairs and a small, dented, tin coffee table. A round-back, white-stitched, fabric couch had a reddish stain that could have been blood. The room had a weird triangle shape. They must have given Lerner a better geometric room than this. I thought I might have trouble sleeping in a triangle, since I was fearful of squares and rectangles from my geometry nightmares. Thank God it had twin beds that were parallel, so I didn't have to sleep with Alan.

The room was way in the back of The Sands, so it took about five minutes to get down to the casino—which was why we came to Vegas: to gamble. We had only $200 but I was excited as we ambled past the slots, craps, poker, and baccarat tables. Alan nervously insisted on roulette first.

"Gol, I know we can win a shitload on red," he said. "Red is my color. Give me five bucks!"

I was carrying our loot and doled out $5 to Alan. The wheel spun round and came up black. Alan insisted on sticking with red—putting us down $10. Finally, I got Alan to follow me to one of the blackjack tables. I'd played a lot of blackjack in Worcester, and I was aiming to apply my skills. I took a seat. On my left was an old lady under a feathery felt hat who looked like she'd been sitting on that wooden stool since The Sands opened. On my right side was a skinny guy with a $5 toupee who was playing $50 chips, smoking regular Camels, tweaking his long black mustache, and draining the ice cubes of a spent Bloody Mary. I looked at the dealer, whose expression said this wasn't going to be a walk in the park. He was shuffling two decks. This was hard core.

Then a cute, twenty-one-year-old, lipsticked, brunette waitress popped up like a target. She had a forever smile and juicy breasts that rested close to her metal tray.

"Sir, what are you drinking?" she asked. Cocktails were always on the house because casino owners like you getting drunk when you play their games.

I promptly responded, "We will have two Seven and Sevens, on the rocks."

That's what we drank in those days—bowls of wet sugar. It was midafternoon and we should have been hitting the strip clubs or stretched out in the desert sun by the pool. But that wasn't to be. Once I sat down at that blackjack table my ass was glued to the seat. I was determined to clean out the house, the house of Sands. Like everyone else in the room, I was a sick gambler ready to lose. The percentages were against me. I knew that, and Alan did, too, but that never stops anyone from doing something stupid.

Alan didn't have the patience to sit at any table—even a family dinner table—and he kept wandering around the casino, talking to anyone who would listen to the shit he made up. Every so often he would stop back and ask me, "How's it going, Gol? Have you lost our $200 yet?"

I had not. In fact, as 6 p.m. approached, I was up about $650. I'd built my Leaning Tower of Pisa stack of Sands chips betting only about $10 on every hand—getting lucky with a pair of aces or kings that I'd split, doubling my bet. And I'd hit a few blackjacks. Back in Worcester I was not considered a great blackjack player. But here I was with $650, a lot of money in 1963. There was no stopping me now.

Time stands still in a casino. As the hours expire it becomes harder and harder for a player to leave that godforsaken, windowless room with its tumbling dice, spinning wheels, shuffling cards, fluttering slots, and waterfalls of change spilling from one-arm bandits. I must have said "Hit me" over a thousand times because the next thing I knew it was 4 a.m. and I had about $5,000 in chips sitting in front of me.

I was drowsily thrilled—so out of it that I could have sworn Dean Martin walked past and waved hello to me, and only me, and warbled, "When the moon hits your eye like a big pizza pie …"

By then I was betting $100 a hand. The cards were hot. I wouldn't admit it then, but I was in way over my head. It was the wee hours when humans got into trouble. My ashtray was full, and the table was empty except for me and a skinny dealer who'd replaced the last wiry dealer. He and I were now playing head-on. I'm sure I bored him to hell, and he'd already been to hell more times than he could count. He wasn't impressed or complimentary about my winnings. But no one in my family had ever held $5,000, even if it was in chips, and I couldn't give a shit what a dealer thought. It represented 25 percent of the value of my parents' house.

Fortunately, not having a clue about the time, I finally had the sense to gather up all my chips. After I left the table, I ran through the lobby and down the corridor. When I got to our room, it was dark. Alan's lights were also off. I found him passed out on the floor, face down with a open bottle of Seagram's 7 in his right hand. I took a swig and dragged him over to the bed. He was soaking wet, sweating like a sumo in a sauna.

"C'mon man, wake up!" I yelled. "We're rich! Look at all these god-damn chips! Look at them, look!" I poured them over his face.

But he was in a deep sleep. The most I could get out of him was a small moan.

For a few minutes I sat on the bedside and thought about calling someone. I didn't think my parents would appreciate my achievement—they'd flip if they knew we were in Vegas gambling and drinking. I don't know why I didn't think to call any of the Crazy Eight, or Irving Kirsch, to tell them I'd beat the goddamn house in Vegas. Nothing could be cooler than that! I could have embellished my feat—told them that I'd been sur-rounded at the blackjack table by showgirls twirling their tassel pasties in my face.

What the hell was I going to do now? Alan probably wouldn't wake up for another eight hours. Sleep was out of the question for me. I was vibrating and all chuffed up. I thought about taking a shower, going for a walk and touring Vegas in a cab. But what was I going to do with the five grand in chips bulging out of my right pants pocket? Then my buzzing brain sent me a message: Go back to the casino! Double your chips! The only reason I'd come back to the room was to get an ego boost from my compadre. That girl who'd told me the reason I was trying to fuck her was so right: We do things because we want to talk about it later.

I raced back down the corridor to the arena I'd just left. I took a deep breath and jumped into the betting pool; now I was going to double the five grand. Man, I was even more excited. I spotted another undernourished dealer at a table without any players. Clean. I sat down and stacked my chips into a sloppy pile. I felt slightly different now. Certainly, I didn't have any natural actuarial talent to calculate my odds. I wasn't an idiot savant who could tell you how many veterinarians practiced in Miami Beach and the probability that they were closed on Wednesday afternoons. I was about to return to the head-spinning netherworld. The gaunt dealer looked at me as if to say, "Buddy, it won't be long before those chips will move across that green felt into my rack."

The first hand, he dealt me two aces. I split them, having put down $100. Now I was in for $200. I was betting that I was going to get a picture card or a high number and be in for $400 right away. Instead, I drew a deuce and a three. There I was sitting with the thirteen and fourteen and afraid to draw another card because I could go over, so I stood pat. The dealer dealt himself a ten and an eight. There went $400 into his chip rack.

The waitress returned with her own large rack.

"Come on, you can touch them," I thought she said. But maybe I heard Dean Martin finishing the song. She was way distracting, and I thought I needed one of those treasured Seven and Sevens to stay on her front side, even though she was working me in the same corporate manner as my dealer, Mr. Emaciated. The drinks followed. He was waiting like a gargoyle for my next wrong move against the deck of life. That was the casino strategy—attack from all sides. I was the innocent target. Three of those drinks later and many sheets to the wind, I was down a grand and fighting to get those chips back like a boxer inside an oversize brown paper bag.

Then I made the move that downhill gamblers make: I began to double my bets. Instead of $100 a pop, I was putting down $200. I was quickly down $2,500. I scratched the curly blond hair of my bowed head. I stared at the melting ice cubes in my cocktail glass. I said, almost out loud, "Why the fuck didn't I stay in the room, take a shower, and go to sleep with my dear chips?" They had got me.

Then there was a change of dealers. Mr. Emaciated was replaced by Mr. Thin As A Rail, another dark-haired, convivial, acne-faced fellow, who seemed to instantly sympathize with me and my losing streak. But wait, didn't I catch him having a whispered word with his departing predecessor? There is nothing worse than a jolt of paranoia when you're on a downswing. I was full of suspicion and desert drinks, as the rest of my chips washed down the rapids of bad luck.

My bloodshot eyes gazed at my last three $25 chips. I felt like a braying donkey had just kicked my ass with both hooves for blowing five grand. I could hear Dirty Art and the rest of the Crazy Eight yelling, "Chopper, what a schmuck! You win the Dumb Shit Award."

That waitress came by to stack the alcohol deck again. She enthusiastically offered another gratis, freshly mixed, effervescent Seven and Seven. The drink's bubbles blurred her huge tits. Her cavern of gleaming white teeth seemed to flash the words, "SEVEN COME ELEVEN"—what you say in craps when you first roll the dice—but she wasn't a pair of dice, she was a pair of tits.

"HIT ME" were the only words on my mind. I could see them as big as the names of the headliners on The Sands marquee. Slowly, I backed away from the table, tucking my tail between my legs. As I waddled to the room with the mummy in residence, I pondered if I should wait for Alan to wake up so I could commune with another human. I needed to undo my guilt, get it off my chest, admit how stupid I'd been to resign from the Quit While You're Ahead Club. Though I wasn't Catholic, I resolved to attend Confession in Room 125.

It wasn't until three in the afternoon that my confessor awakened.

"Gol, how'd you do?" Alan asked, trying to open his eyes.

There is something seedy about losing at night and having to explain yourself in the raw afternoon, in a humid hotel room in Las Vegas. My only solace was I wasn't the first or last to do that.

I didn't have to say much for Alan to figure out the night hadn't gone well. The good thing was that he didn't care. He really didn't care about anything, anything at all. He was the ultimate life gambler, everything happened by chance. You will rarely meet anyone like that.

"Gol, I see you lost," he said, sucking the smoke from a filter-tipped Marlboro. "Now what's the plan?" The past meant nothing.

We still had the little matter of our bill, which we now had little or no way of paying. The miserable night before, I'd noticed that the window at the end of our corridor had bars on it—apparently so that guests like us couldn't climb out and scoot down the alley to escape without paying. No, you had to pass right by the front desk and pay the line. And I was sure the hulking piper, Jack Entratter, would like a word with us, and he wouldn't be speaking in the same tone he accorded Mr. Frank Sinatra. He might even send one of his snub-nosed "customer relations" specialists to deal with us.

There must have been a reasonable way out of this, but I was twenty years old and my brain was still in the slow process of maturing. Plus,

I detested this city where Jack Entratter, and others, made millions off suckers like me.

"I'd love to blow this fucking place up," I blurted out.

I suddenly had an idea.

It started with a variation on our exit strategy at the Stephen F. Austin Motel in Texas. First, we artfully left our suitcases in the lobby of The Sands. Then, we asked the parking valet to fetch our car. Once the car had arrived and was idling in the driveway, Alan set fire to a brown paper bag. After igniting this bag, Alan walked casually away and yelled, "Fire!"

Mind you, this wasn't just any brown paper bag. It contained four pounds of cherry bombs. Obviously, this plan was modeled after the cherry bomb event which had gotten me bounced out of Worcester Academy in 1957. Everyone has a pattern and here mine was again. I now viewed myself not as a wise-ass preppy but as a seasoned pyrotechnologist. My behavior was as reliable as a Swiss watch.

A few seconds after Alan's fire alarm, the contents of the bag started blowing up—one bomb after another.

The front desk clerk and the bellmen ran toward the explosions, as we slowly walked out the front door with our ratty suitcases. We slipped into the black Dodge Dart, top down, and lit out for Los Angeles. I drove as fast as I could to get the hell out of Nevada; our brush with the law in Texas still had me paranoid. Just up ahead on the highway, in my mind, I saw a police roadblock—it was always there, fixed in the distance. My paranoia got us to California in no time.

CHAPTER 13:

Into the lap of Hollywood

As we approached LA, we were greeted by a thick wet smog that must have been hanging over the city since the Second World War. The forecast, on KLAX, was for light rain, clearing in the afternoon. It was 6 a.m., John Wayne—"The Duke"—was probably sleeping through the drizzle at his hacienda up the road, with all the others whom God had star-blessed.

We were aiming for Hollywood but, thanks again to my family's screwy sense of direction, we wound up in downtown LA. Randomly, we parked near the dilapidated stucco Greyhound Bus terminal, at Sixth and Los Angeles Street. The place was haunted by a pack of hungry, howling, stray dogs. A sign near the boarding area warned, "Don't miss the bus! Bad things can happen to you." That's right, LA welcomed you with the feeling that something terrible could happen at any moment.

We ate a meager breakfast from the terminal's vending machines, then wandered outside, pushing through a chorus line of panhandlers—dustbowl characters, some discarded ranch hands. They regarded us as high society, calling us "Sir" and "Mister," which felt weird. It took us a few hours to get our bearings. Our lodestar was the HOLLYWOOD sign, high on Mount Lee.

Tired as we were, there was too much to see. We were in goddamned Hollywood! I'd waited all my life for this moment—having learned everything about the entertainment industry from our Admiral black-and-white TV, in the basement of 28 Wamsutta Avenue.

Finding ourselves in Beverly Hills, we headed up Sunset Boulevard, the revered thoroughfare that all Angelinos grind, east and west, every day. When we hit La Brea, we pulled over at a sign for "Star Maps." A ten-year-old Mexican kid, wearing a large sombrero and a Clint Eastwood-size blue poncho, was hustling them. He said each map contained 100 reliable celebrity addresses. The farther west we went, the more Mexicans we met. I bought one, for two bucks, and unfolded it on the hood of the car. My index finger floated over the homes of Claudette Colbert, Gary Cooper, Clark Gable, Myrna Loy, and lots of current stars. Shit, I was so bloated with possibilities I thought I was going to throw up.

We drove straight to Bel Air, romping up and down its hilly streets. The neighborhood was a paradise, but most of the houses were hidden behind stone walls, tall hedges, huge gates, and driveways that wound around to nowhere. There was a shitload of "No Trespassing" signs with scary lettering—as though people like us really obeyed signs that were sold in the hardware store.

While we were snooping around, an old song came on the car radio: "Be My Love," by Mario Lanza.

"I'll bet he lived in Beverly Hills," I said.

"No doubt," said Alan. "Beverly Hills. Or Bel Air. He was a huge star."

I looked, again, at our map and, sure enough, there was a tiny photo of Mario Lanza—his mouth wide open in song.

"Hey," I said, "Mario's house is at 355 St. Cloud Road, Bel Air."

"Wait," Alan said. "Is he still alive? Didn't he die?"

"I don't know. Let's check it out anyway," I said.

We sped down Sunset, taking a right into the second Bel Air Gate, singing a duet of "Be My Love."

355 St. Cloud turned out to be a vast white, Mediterranean house, protected by high brick walls and double iron gates. It looked strangely inviting, and yet even at 10 a.m., in the misty morning light, haunted.

Now that we were there, what was next? After all the driving, we were tired. As usual, we had no place to stay. I got out of the car, stretched, thinking I might ring the bell and ask if anyone was home. Then I noticed that the gate was ajar. I pushed it open with one finger and started ambling up the wide, oleander-lined driveway. Alan sidled up alongside me. We followed the driveway, under an archway, into the backyard. The house didn't look lived in. The grass and shrubbery hadn't been cut, the garden was full of weeds and thriving digitalis. There were no cars and no sounds. Alan wandered around the empty swimming pool.

"I'm going to find the tennis court," he said. He didn't play tennis, but he loved to wear white shorts.

I looked through a set of French doors. I pushed one and it swung open. Inside, I found an enormous living room with beige carpeting and a grand dining room, where a lot of pasta with meat sauce had been served. Neither room had furniture. Clearly, not a soul had been in this house for some time.

Standing in front of a large, decorative, concrete fireplace, I belted out a few verses of "Be My Love"—complete with hand gestures. Just when I was reaching a nice crescendo, Alan came strolling in.

"Gol, this is it!" he enthused, "the real thing, Mario's house! You know how I love opera."

He did love what he thought was opera. He rightfully considered both *Oklahoma!* and *Much Ado About Nothing* operas. I disagreed, but what did I know?

I pulled the car into the driveway, hiding it behind the house. Coming back inside, I heard Alan running around all the bedrooms as if they were bases on a ball diamond. Primitive man had nothing on him. He came scampering down the staircase, swinging on its wrought iron railings like a gymnast on parallel bars.

"The water is shut off and the lights don't work," he reported, as excited as a Mario Lanza, opening night, first-row, ticket holder. "But there are beds! I tried them and they are good as new, very sleepable."

In the breakfast room I found a copy of a 1959, front-page *Los Angeles Times* story headlined, "LANZA DEAD AT 38 OF APPARENT HEART ATTACK." A real estate broker's card was stapled to it. I handed the clipping to Alan.

"At least we know Mario's not coming home," I said.

"I didn't know he drank so much," Alan said, skimming the story. "And that he ate like a pig."

"That's what killed him," I said. "Keep reading. He must have been unhappy."

I thought about the night I'd taken Deeny Yudell to that Boston strip joint and how she said that dancer must be happier than we were. Breaking into Mario's home felt good, it made me happier than any stripper could. I also felt damn rude; the man could carry a tune.

Then again, this was a cool place to hang out. It was yet another thing we could tell our friends.

For the next two nights we camped out in that mansion. We lit candles and slept with the French doors open. We enjoyed the sweet eucalyptus-scented Bel Air air—the same air that the very rich breathed.

There were other houses I was bent on invading. When I was fourteen, I'd discovered architecture— partly to blaze a cultural path that would rival Linda's artistic ambitions. Frank Lloyd Wright had always fascinated me. One of my big dreams was to live in the house he designed, for Charles and Mabel Ennis, in 1923. It looked like a Mayan temple. I'd read that no one currently lived there.

"Alan," I said, "there's this incredible house in a place called Los Feliz. I want to see it."

"I thought we were just going to hang out on St. Cloud tonight," he grumbled.

"This is more than a house," I said. "It's a wonder of the world—and it's empty. Maybe we can even get in."

That's all Alan needed to hear. We were off. For the hell of it, we drove down Hollywood Boulevard, where pimps, whores, and drugstore cowboys strut across the gold sidewalk stars, on the Walk of Fame, all day and all night. Just like Times Square in the West. We really wanted to stop at Musso & Frank Grill, the famous Jewish deli, to have a hot dog with sauerkraut and to get the honest feel of Hollywood. But we were on a mission.

It took us a half hour to get to the Ennis House. It was dark inside. The weather-beaten exterior was deteriorating. I felt sorry for Frank Lloyd Wright, because his masterpiece was in such disrepair. It must have been difficult to build that sucker on such a steep hill. It was a real engineering feat. The house overlooked Los Angeles—the best damn city-lights view money could buy.

For a while, we just stared at the place like it was Godzilla. Then we walked to the padlocked gates.

"Well, Gol," Alan grinned, "should we give it a shot?"

Having proposed this escapade, I was now put off by the intimidating monolith. A chill crawled up my spine.

"You mean, try to get in?" I asked, not so sure.

By then, Alan was already down the street, climbing a wall. I soon joined him. The side of the house had staggered levels of concrete blocks.

You had to get to the top of one wall, then scale another. Finally, we reached the top.

"Shit," I said, looking down on a lit-up, aquamarine pool, where I could imagine Esther Williams swimming laps. "You're right, we have to get inside."

"You bet," he affirmed. "This couldn't be more fabulous!"

We'd just set foot inside the wall, when four ferocious Doberman pinschers sprang from the shadows—snarling, barking, baring their teeth. I began scrambling back up the wall with Alan. It was lucky we weren't on the patio. It would've meant no escape, no more Linda or Woonsocket. The gardener would've found our bones in the morning.

We drove back to Mario's mansion but, by our third day there, we were getting tired of no water and no lights. The place was free, but it was depressing. We couldn't go on squatting, even though it was our stock in trade. Sooner or later, someone would discover us. And I couldn't give UCLA summer school my address as, "the late Mario Lanza's house."

* * *

No, we needed to find new digs. When we were crossing the great Southwest, during one of my roadside pay-phone calls to home, my mother reminded me that we had relatives in LA—rich relatives. My cousin Gert was married to Walter Maier, a stocky Austrian, who'd brought his wavy hair and simmering temper from Innsbruck. Walter worked in Leominster, Massachusetts, with Gert's brother, Sam Foster. Sam was an inventor, who founded a pioneering plastic molding company with a guy named Bill Grant. FosterGrant originally specialized in women's hair accessories but later moved into making sunglasses. Once, only blind people wore sunglasses, but gradually, movie stars helped make FosterGrant shades popular. In 1942, Sam and Walter headed out to the land of movie stars and went into the real estate business—leaving the sunglasses to Sam's son, in Massachusetts.

Once, Walter visited us in Worcester. He was affable but stern. Back then, he said to me, "If you ever come to Los Angeles, I will show you around." It was a riskless proposition for him because I was just ten and not likely to go anywhere near California. Besides, Walter wouldn't have been my tour guide of choice; I'd have gone for Mickey Mouse or Donald Duck. But I liked his brunette wife, Gert. She was a lithe, short, thin thing of a woman, who talked like a scientist and acted like a Vanderbilt. She was from the Kaplan side of the family, all of whom have a birdlike quality. She could be condescending, but she was quite gracious when making the short flight down to my kid level.

Ten years later, and I was in LA. At first, I wasn't inclined to look them up. I didn't want to sit at a dining room table behaving like a good relative. And how would I control Alan? But I'd seen photos of the Maiers' spread. They had a big house with a swimming pool. I dialed their number.

Gert was surprised to hear that I'd car-tripped across the USA and had brought a New England companion. She asked why I didn't tell them sooner that I was going to summer school at UCLA. Ingratiatingly, I said we didn't want to disturb them—that is, until now, when, in fact, we were dying to disturb them.

She courteously invited us over for dinner. The following night, we pulled up to their house at 11559 Sunset Boulevard in Brentwood. Gert and Walter welcomed us and introduced us to their daughters, Susan and Linda. The girls were about our age—cool, nice-looking, and friendly. Gert and Walter loved the idea that I was attending UCLA and getting college credits. And, since they really liked my parents, they were sympathetic to my need for student housing. They told us they were leaving, the next day, for two weeks in Lake Tahoe. They invited us to stay in their pool house—or, as they called it, the cabana. Alan and I were on a hot streak!

That week I had to register at UCLA. Driving to the campus, we stopped at a traffic light at Sunset and Royce Drive. I looked over to the brand-new, ice green Cadillac convertible, with cream leather seats, idling to my left. Sitting behind the wheel was actor John Gavin, who'd recently starred in *Spartacus, Psycho*, and *Imitation of Life*. Gavin's hair was slicked back, perfectly, and he wore a light, matching green cotton sports jacket. In retrospect, he must have been out for a Hollywood star ride, to show himself off to the LA public. To me, he seemed bored at the stoplight. Then again, to me, he looked like a million bucks whatever his motivation. I thought, "Damn, he's got the world by the balls!"

"Hey, John!" I yelled.

He cast a bothered movie star glance my way.

I asked him, "Where is a good place to hang out in Los Angeles?"

Glaring right at me, he suggested: "See a psychiatrist."

Then he roared off.

Alan and I weren't insulted so much as tongue-tied. How had he known that—based on our cross-country hijinks—we probably needed psychoanalysis? Years later I learned that, though his pal Ronald Reagan appointed him ambassador to Mexico (WASPy John Gavin was born Juan Vincent Apablasa), he didn't fulfill his early promise and resented being called "the poor man's Rock Hudson." I should have told *him* to see a shrink, and about all the other Mexicans we met on the trip.

I enrolled in Introductory Spanish and Development of Jazz. The courses were dirt cheap—seventy-five bucks for three credits per course, just enough to meet Clark University's senior year requirements.

Classes started the next day. As soon as I reported to Spanish class, I was struck by the Venezuelan beauty who was my Spanish professor. After a couple of classes, I confessed to her that Spanish was killing me. I just couldn't unravel verb conjugations. She offered to tutor me in the afternoons. Of course, I had an ulterior motive. We were building a solid relationship, when I learned she had a boyfriend and I abandoned all hope of conjugating with her. I used my Development of Jazz homework to take out my frustration—arhythmically beating my bongos late into the night.

There wasn't a hell of a lot of homework, so, almost every night Alan and I went out. When we returned home, we wouldn't go straight to the cabana; instead, we'd go right to the big house and party. Over the next two weeks, we drained Walter's well-stocked bar of about $2,000 worth of wine and spirits. We left one lonely bottle of Johnny Walker Red and a six-pack of Budweiser.

When the Maiers returned home, Walter was naturally upset about the missing booze. He immediately kicked us off the property—but in a classy way. When he calmed down, he said, "The wine can be replaced." Then he offered me a job.

"Richard," he said, "you know, I own eighty-two Texaco stations in the Los Angeles area; you could work part-time at one after school."

"I accept. When do I start?"

"Next week. You can drive out there and speak to the manager. You know how to pump gas and you know about car engines, I presume."

"Of course, I do," I lied.

So it was that I wound up driving to Glendale every day to don a drab green, Texaco gas jockey uniform and hat. The outfit made me sweat like a desert legionnaire. Self-service was in the future, but I didn't tell. So, I was at the customers' mercy— squeegeeing windshields and holding that fucking pump hose while I watched the number of gallons roll, slowly, around and around.

Almost every day, some customer would tell me they heard "a funny noise" in the engine.

"Can you take a look?" the customer would ask.

"Happy to," I'd smile, teeth gritted.

I usually couldn't even open the hood; customers would need to help me. It made them angry, but they would do it. After listening to the mysterious rattle like a recording engineer, I would tell them that, professionally speaking, "It could just be anything." I would give them a list of possible problems—"might be the carburetor," "might be the distributor"—none of which I could fix. Instead of referring them to our garage mechanic, I would tell them to go down the road to a repair shop. In a matter of weeks, I was fired and Walter wouldn't hear of hiring me back.

* * *

I'd gotten into the habit of reading *The Hollywood Reporter*. One day I saw that *Cleopatra* was opening that afternoon. Everyone was talking about this movie, which starred Liz Taylor and Richard Burton. Nothing was bigger except the World Series.

"Alan, let's get down to Hollywood Boulevard and see some stars," I said. "We've never been to an opening. One like this will never happen again!"

The news had Alan almost foaming at the mouth.

"Nothing could be more fabulous," he agreed. "Let's crash it!"

When we got to Hollywood and Vine, we found the block barricaded. LAPD cops were everywhere. You couldn't get through unless you had a VIP pass.

I took a sharp left off Hollywood and up to Yucca Street. We parked in someone's driveway, under a dead palm tree. We didn't care if we got towed. We were bursting with excitement. I loved Elizabeth Taylor in *Cat on a Hot Tin Roof*. I imagined being Paul Newman looking into her violet eyes. I kept a version of Richard Burton's Welsh accent in my arsenal of posh dialects.

We marched down the hill and scoured the area for a way to penetrate the Hollywood Pantages Theatre. It was a formidable no-go. Security centurions stood, shoulder-to-shoulder, at every entrance. Standing, dejectedly, in a parking lot behind the theater, I suddenly noticed a metal door about chest high.

"Check this out," I said, pulling Alan by the hand. The door had a handle and, when we tugged it, it opened like a desk drawer.

"Damn, Gol," Alan whispered. "It's a laundry chute."

Like prisoners headed to freedom, we climbed in. The next thing I knew we were coasting down a slide in the dark. We landed on top of each other on a mountain of dirty clothes.

Minutes later, we were up the steps and inside the theater—right on the stage, hiding behind red velvet curtains. I peeked out and saw ushers busily showing guests to their seats. And there, in the second bank of seats, were Elizabeth and Richard! Incredibly, right next to them were two empty seats. I looked at Alan. No sooner did our eyes meet than we were on our way to those empty seats.

As we sat down, I said, "Miss Taylor, may I introduce my friend, Alan Golden?"

"Your *what*?" she croaked.

Cleopatra motioned for an underling. An usher promptly walked over and asked for our invitations. With no Aspray, Lerner, or other fake name to fall back on, we were hustled out a side door and shoved into an alley. The premiere went on without us.

* * *

The next day, we headed west. We were searching, not for a shrink as John Gavin had suggested, but for an apartment around UCLA. We finally relented to paying rent. Well, our parents were paying. Needing a place near school, we cruised Westwood, meeting weird rental managers who'd had their acting dreams crushed by the movie business. After checking countless kitchens and bathrooms, with '40s tiles and fixtures, we landed at 625 Landfair Avenue, a large apartment complex, with a rocky, glazed façade, on a hill. Its manager, a seventy-plus woman named Mrs. Hughes, was sitting on a lawn chair smoking a fresh cigarette. A sizable butt was still glowing in the ashtray. Alan loved talking to old ladies and now he had a cool one to chatter away with. Right away, he affectionately dubbed her Huggie and they bonded. Since I grew up with my two grandmothers, I knew the granny routine inside and out. The three of us bonded, and then we rented right away. We established our headquarters in Unit 1A, right off the barren, concrete courtyard.

Across the street was the Pi Kappa Phi frat house. We greeted some of the bare-chested brothers throwing a football on the front lawn. They seemed cool and the neighborhood was full of UCLA students. But what did I know then about what was cool in Los Angeles? This was a bin of transplanted wannabes, where even ordinary people hoped and prayed to be mistaken for actors. I thought I'd made it from Worcester to Hollywood, the glossy castle where stars were assembled. But I was only in Westwood, a prelude—not the beer, more like near beer.

As always, I was bound and determined to get inside the Hollywood castle.

That June I met Susan Bensman, another UCLA student. We went out for about a month. Susan's short-bodied, large-headed uncle, Si Howard, was in the TV and movie business. He invited us to Paramount Studios the following week. Suddenly, I was on a film set! All my dreams of seeing stars were coming true. All I had to do was stand there. George Peppard walked past me wearing a strange costume and a smile. HHe was rehearsing for *The Carpetbaggers*, someone said.

Paramount was shooting a movie called *For Those Who Think Young*, a college comedy starring James Darren, Pamela Tiffin, Paul Lynde, Nancy

Sinatra, Ellen Burstyn, Bob Denver, and George Raft. Most importantly to me, it featured Tina Louise. I'd had a crush on Tina since I watched the sun radiate between those incredible legs through her transparent cotton dress in the film, *God's Little Acre*. That was when I was sixteen; now she was in front of me—playing saucy Topaz McQueen, walking around in a red ball gown. I followed her, thinking she might lead me to the promised land. Finally, when she stopped to get coffee, I circled around and asked her out,

"Tina," I ventured, "what are you doing tonight? Would you like to go to dinner?"

She looked me up and down and politely laughed.

"I already have a date tonight," she said. "And I'm not even going to ask your name, although I know you have one."

Those two dismissive sentences were much more than I expected. I was thrilled to have pocketed a rejection from Tina Louise. Twenty years later, I would wind up dating her and becoming her mother's lawyer in a crazy case. But, for now, it was enough of an adventure to try to pick up a movie star so I could tell my friends in Worcester.

If Tina had gone out to dinner with me, she might have doused my Linda flames for good. As it was, I hadn't placed one phone call to Linda, or received one, since we'd hit Los Angeles. I did hear from our mutual friend Debbie Gross that Linda was in Rome—on one of those tour groups for rich kids that I'd seen in travel magazines. She was probably walking around the Colosseum, stuffing a focaccia in her mouth. There was no way to reach her except through her horrific mother or deadly brother. Calling her house was out. It would have been Princess phone electrocution.

Besides, I'd put her out of my mind, momentarily, because Alan and I were having such a great, wild summer. Days were a little mellower. When I was in class, Alan hung out at our apartment, combing his hair, looking in the mirror, telling himself jokes, hanging out with Huggie, and walking around Westwood. Alan would often do the "shopping"—which meant walking into a Safeway and stuffing bloody rib-eyes into the waistband of his white pants. We also stole a bigger piece of aged meat from the frat house across the street. The brothers had mounted a huge moose head over the sitting room fireplace. Late one night, we moved "Moose" to our place. Afterward, we often took him out for some sightseeing. Moose sat in the back seat as we drove around LA with the top down.

There was a lot to do in Los Angeles and we were not going to permit any slack in that department. We had a program. Just about every night, we went to 525 Perugia Way, right off Bellagio Road, where the taste of fresh Bel Air money is right in your face. Elvis was living there in a long ranch-style rental. I think he was shooting *Viva Las Vegas*. We hung out across the street for hours, waiting like groupies, for Elvis and Ann-Margret to emerge. When they did, they were ringed by Elvis' pal-bodyguards, the Memphis Mafia, clad in their mohair suits.

I had only one idol and it was Elvis. My adulation was based on facts. Fact One: I'd seen him the first time he performed on TV—twitching like a roach on a blowtorch. Fact Two: Elvis fired a bullet into his 25-inch RCA TV while watching Robert Goulet perform. Fact Three: Elvis slipped the name Linda into "Don't Be Cruel." ("Let's walk to the preacher and let us say 'I do' / Then you're gonna have me and I know, Linda, I'll have you…") That must have been a fifties Linda, pre-Linda Thompson. I don't think it was Worcester's Linda Paul.

* * *

While I was in LA I wasn't exactly faithful to Linda. Why should I be, considering the evolving Paul-Gordon matrix? Plus, there were many temptations. The UCLA coeds made Worcester girls look like tugboat captains. One of those women walked past our building on Landfair Avenue every day at 3 p.m. She wore a short, navy-blue knit skirt that the breeze regularly lifted, exposing her white, cotton underwear. It was far sexier than the scene in *Some Like It Hot* where the passing subway car blows Marilyn Monroe's dress up.

I made it my business to be at our kitchen window whenever that girl walked by. Finally, I got sick of just watching. It was time to make my move. Strolling outside, when her skirt was at half-mast, I introduced myself.

"Hi," I said nervously. "My name is Richard Golub. I'm from Massachusetts and I go to UCLA summer school."

She flashed a beautiful, red-lipstick grin.

"I go to UCLA, too!" she said. "My name is Donna Kling."

After we spoke for a few minutes, I invited her into the apartment for coffee. We established that we shared a bad habit: Marlboro Filter Tips. That was a good start, although I had a better use for her lips in mind. I was so excited I felt like I had been elected to do this job. This girl was knocking me out. Donna was major league—Linda was Little League.

Once inside, she sat on our gamey living room couch—a goddess on a garbage can—and didn't complain. Thank God, Alan wasn't around. He was probably at the Westwood Safeway shoplifting.

"Do you have a match?" she asked, holding her Marlboro between her long fingers, skirt hiked up to her tanned thighs. She was making me feel weird. Here she was, right off the sidewalk, in the palm of my hand, and all I could say to myself was "Don't fuck this up!"

I went into the kitchen to get a match. Damn if I could find one. I looked everywhere for a light, even in the fridge. I tried turning on the range burners—the pilots didn't seem to be working. Next, I turned on the gas oven. It wasn't igniting, so I stuck my head inside to sort out the problem. Before I could render my professional opinion, I heard gas jets clicking like castanets. Then *whoosh* and BANG! The oven blew up in my face. Jumping backward, I saw that my eyebrows and arm hair were scorched. Sniffing something foul like a fowl, I realized my head was ablaze. I was still snuffing out the flames with a dish towel as I walked back into the living room, but I got the cigarette lit. I tried to be suave, handing her the blackened cigarette that had been in my mouth when the inferno erupted. At least I'd gotten *that* lit.

"What was that noise?" she asked. "Are you … are you alright?"

I was touched by her concern.

"Sure, I'm fine," I answered, trying to pull myself together.

Clearly, she knew something crazy had happened in the kitchen. But that didn't deter me from making my move. Planting myself next to her on the sofa, I asked, "Are you busy tonight?"

"No, I'm not," she said. "I would love to go out. Say… do you smell burning chicken?"

I didn't answer. My personal aroma was pungent, but I told myself the kitchen explosion must have impressed her. Perhaps it was something I should work into my standard pickup routine.

We set a time for dinner. As she walked out of the apartment, I studied her as if she were a painting, like Venus on the half-shell, hanging on my wall. Linda's Lothario, Gordon, couldn't snag a woman like this with two red Corvettes and first-row seats at the Indianapolis Speedway.

Promptly at eight, I swung by her place. I'd cleaned myself up— slicking back my singed hair in a wave. Donna slipped into the passenger seat. She was wearing a short white linen dress. It didn't look like she had on anything underneath. I asked her if she had an exemption from the California State Department of Underwear.

We went to dinner in a divey Sunset Boulevard hamburger joint that had a decent jukebox. Sucking on our sodas with long straws, we stared at each other like two lovesick immigrants helping one another through customs. I suggested we ride up to Griffith Observatory on Mount Hollywood. Two scenes in *Rebel Without a Cause* were filmed there. There was no better place to fulfill a Hollywood fantasy. Donna eagerly agreed, and we were off to James Dean Land with my hard-on pointing the way.

Driving over, I suggested we stop at the Ennis House, where Alan and I had narrowly escaped those fanged Dobermans. Lit up now, the house looked less threatening. I gave my short lecture on Frank Lloyd Wright and Mayan architecture. Donna seemed impressed, which was good. I wanted to warm up her brain before I went for her body. We proceeded to Griffith Park, up the winding road to the observatory. We parked. No other cars were around. It was like the make-out area at Worcester's Bancroft Tower magnified to the 100th power.

The starry sky was clear, just like my head that intended to go all the way. Soon we were furiously kissing. Donna's lips were softer and more experienced than Linda's. I hadn't even said anything romantic when she began peeling off her clothes. This was another world, one of the body beautiful. In no time at all, my fantasy girl was lying across my lap, stark naked, as if I'd ordered takeout and it had been delivered.

"Do you want to make love to me?" she whispered.

In that moment, my dick could have been as long and hard as the observatory's telescope. But I'd made a tragic mistake—I'd left the radio on. Suddenly, I heard a song: "Stranger in Paradise." Fucking Tony Bennett was crooning his way into this once-in-a-lifetime situation, just as he'd done in Linda's rumpus room when she danced me around her easel with her arms wrapped around my neck. Now it felt like Linda was choking me. Through the windshield I saw Linda, staring at me—a grinning witch waving her finger back and forth, admonishing me not to make it with Donna. If I did, she would find out and that would be the end of us—even if our relationship was close to the finish line, with Gordon waving the checkered flag.

My erection took a nosedive.

As feeble as it could get, I said to Donna, "Ahhh, tonight's too beautiful. Let's wait until next time."

Even as the words walked off my lips I wondered, who the hell just said that? The old Linda knot in my head had done me in again. I tried to fudge it by telling Donna about self-deprivation and abstinence. I assured her that, if we waited, we'd really fall deeply in love.

"The next time will be amazing," I exclaimed. Then I said, "The bird in the bush is better than one in hand." Yes, I said that.

The pun made her wince.

"Are you a Buddhist?" she asked. "Are you celibate?"

I didn't answer. I'd shriveled from a lover into a philosopher. The goddess quickly got dressed. We sat there silently, gazing at the sky for thirty minutes. But the answer was not in our stars.

I drove her home. When we arrived at her apartment house, I went balls out and told her that I'd been "defrocked"—kicked out of a religious order. I apologized for our unhappy misunderstanding. I asked for another chance, a date the following weekend, when, I vowed, I would be ready for love.

Curiously, she seemed to buy my bullshit. She said she'd be going home next weekend, to Laguna Beach to see her parents, but that she'd very much like to see me again if I wanted to drive down.

With the welcome mat rolled out down the 405 Interstate, I imagined we'd go to the beach with a blanket, like that time with the babysitter who took my virginity. I wasn't going to mess up again. All the way back home, I cursed myself like a soused wino on welfare for screwing up on Mount Hollywood.

On Friday afternoon, I hauled down to Laguna in a sweltering heat. Again, I was packing a stiff bulge. Once I got to Orange County, I pulled over and called her from a pay phone. For two hours, there was no answer. It was very similar to Linda's phone etiquette, so I was well prepped for that treatment. Around 8:30 p.m., just as I was ready to abandon date #2, Donna's mother picked up. Sounding suspiciously like Donna, she informed me that Donna had just had her wisdom teeth removed and was in bed, unable to come to the phone.

* * *

When I got back to Landfair Avenue, Alan was sitting in the kitchen with his nose buried in a magazine called *Palm Springs Life*.

"How was your date?" he asked, dousing a cigarette in a coffee cup. "Fabulous?"

I was still upset about Donna, the trip to Orange County, and how I'd blown it.

"What are you doing reading that?" I asked him. "Are you planning to move to the desert?"

"Gol, I can see it on your face—you didn't have the good time you thought you were going to have. Did she stand you up?"

I understood jealousy and condoned it if it wasn't dangerous. But Alan never competed with me when it came to women. Usually, he was an ally. He wanted me to have what he could only have in his dreams.

"This will cheer you up," he said, offering me the magazine. "Look at all the great things to do in Palm Springs. We can play tennis, golf, and get lost in the desert with rich people from Los Angeles. We can socialize!"

"Socialize? With rich people? All we do is see the outside of their houses. We don't get any closer than a bus driver."

"Look, if we go to Palm Springs, I guarantee you we will meet rich people. I'm good at that and so are you. There is no place we will get thrown out of this time."

"Then I guess the first stop will be the Chamber of Commerce. I'm sure they'll help with the introductions."

"Palm Springs is going to be fabulous. These pictures tell a story, and it's a good one for us. I know I will fit in."

Alan stood up, walked into the living room, opened the closet, took out his small suitcase, and started packing a few of his best items.

Late the next day, wanting to put the Donna disappointment behind me, I got in the car. Off we went east to the desert. There wasn't much to see on Route 111. At one point, Alan muttered something about doing an impossible stunt. We were cruising at 60 mph, top down, when we pulled alongside a car driven by a beautiful, twenty-something blond. She looked like a surfer girl. Alan looked like the classic surfer boy. Women couldn't resist his wind-swept platinum mop and his forever smile. This blond was his match in heaven.

"Hey, baby," he yelled, motioning her to roll down her window. "Where you headed?"

"Bonnie," she screamed without hesitation, though he hadn't asked her name.

"I'm an actress!" she added. "An actress!"

Over the next high-speed miles, with the desert wind throttling his cheeks, Alan reeled in Bonnie's phone number.

As she sped off, Alan cackled, "Just shows you, Gol—all you have to do is open your mouth, at any speed, and you can hit the jackpot. She couldn't wait to tell me she was Bonnie the actress. And I'm Alan from Woonsocket."

"I thought she was going to say, 'My name is Jack,'" I laughed. "'You know me—Jack the Ripper!'"

Rolling into Palm Springs, we cruised around for a while. Hours passed and Alan didn't mention Bonnie. Weren't we supposedly there to meet new people? I figured that was his way of being cool, but this was a little too cool.

"Why don't you try to hook up with her tonight," I demanded to know if he'd make a move.

There was no immediate response. He just stared at the road; speechlessly looking at wide-open spaces or objects was another Alan characteristic that I just accepted as part of the general fun of being with him.

"Gol, I'm hungry," he finally said.

This was his subject changer. When I was chasing a woman, I could go for days without food or sleep. But Alan always claimed to be hungry. He ate like a pig and never gained a pound.

"Let's go *there*," he said excitedly, pointing to The Pancake House. It had a huge neon sign that showed maple syrup cascading onto a pile of buttered flapjacks. I usually liked to first find a place to stay and get settled. But I gave in.

We sat down at the counter. It was 10 p.m. and there weren't any other customers in the place. I studied the menu, trying to find something other than pancakes with dessert toppings. When I looked up, Alan was gone.

I checked the bathroom and surveyed the parking lot. No Alan. I went back to the counter. I'd just compromised on blueberry pancakes with mixed nuts and strawberry syrup when Alan materialized.

"Gol, do not turn around … yet," he grinned.

"Why not? What's going on?"

"Wait five minutes, go to the car, and look in the trunk."

After I ordered, I went out to the car. Opening the trunk, I saw three wooden cases of California Merlot. I looked in the back seat, three more cases were seated like errant passengers. I was shocked. Breaking into houses was far different from *stealing*, a famous person should have once said.

Back at the counter, Alan was perusing the menu, calm as a frog on a lily pad.

I whispered, "Where the hell did you get that wine?"

"The bulkhead to the basement was open," he reluctantly disclosed.

"I just lost my appetite," I said. "Let's get the fuck out of here."

"I just ordered buttermilk pancakes with strawberries," Alan insisted. "I'm starving!"

As we sat there, I thought about the thousands of dollars' worth of wine that was sitting in my car. The thought that we would be busted turned over in my head like a rotisserie chicken. Like that chicken, my flushed face dripped with greasy sweat. Alan seemed unaffected as he wolfed down his pancakes. I went out to the car to protect it. Finally, Alan moseyed out with a toothpick between his teeth and hopped in. He told me how much he liked eating pancakes at night.

We argued vehemently about staying in Palm Springs. Alan wanted to find a cheap motel—something I was sure didn't exist in this ritzy enclave. I also didn't want to stick around with this hot cargo in my car. It was getting late, but I prevailed. We headed back to Los Angeles.

Two hundred and twenty miles later, we pulled into our garage. Even though I was exhausted, and pissed at Alan, I wanted to see and feel the wine. After all, we didn't have the bucks to buy a good bottle. We ripped open the first case, then the second, then the third. They were all filled with empty bottles of Napa Valley wine that had been re-corked. We'd duped ourselves. I sat there thinking that it was about time we got our just deserts.

Donna, my goddess, vanished. Maybe she went back to Mount Olympus. To add insult to self-injury, the chiseled brothers of Pi Kappa Phi paid us a visit. Not bothering to knock, they barged into the living room where Alan was sitting with his arm around our constant companion, Moose. Seconds later, Moose was gone. I almost broke down in tears, but Alan actually cried. He loved Moose, and I think the feeling was mutual.

CHAPTER 14:

Back to Reality

By mid-August, summer school was over. I'd gotten my credits and there was no reason for Alan and me to stick around. LA was a circular environment: After a few weeks we kept repeating the same pattern—cruising up and down the hills and back and forth on Sunset like everyone else in LA. In LA, every person I knew ate at 6 p.m. and went to bed by 9 p.m. It was time to say goodbye to Huggie, and to abandon the land of false gods and heroes. Our large teary sob of departure stretched from Sunset Strip to the Nevada state line. It was a hell of a summer, but aren't all summers supposed to be wild when you're a kid? There is one time to do this road trip, and now it had been done. Did we mature? Did we discover anything about the meaning of life? I would submit in the negative, but one thing I dragged along with my shallowness: Someday I would return to Los Angeles and dig deeper into the emptiness.

Envisioning the trip back, I felt it wouldn't be that eventful. There would be no Stephen F. Austin Motels, no brothels. This time we would take the northern route but, otherwise, it would be a simple reversal of America. Going up the piano octave, would now be an arpeggio back down to middle C. We were going nowhere except where the tar carpet called Route 66 would lead us.

As things turned out, we quickly ran into misfortune. We walked out of a diner in Nevada, leaving a leather pouch with most of our money on the counter. Maybe it was because I was freaked out by the counter waitress, the one that had a thick black beard that hung down to her pointed breasts. That fifty bucks would've gotten us to the Midwest.

We drove fast and slept in the car and called home for Western Union bucks. Just like on the way west, Alan did most of the sleeping. In Nebraska, where there was nothing but flat farmland, I opened it up to 110 mph and got stopped. Alan woke up in time to see me tried for speeding inside a gas station garage. The judge happened to be the station's owner. His robe was an oil-stained gas jockey uniform. He also wore a Boston Red Sox baseball cap. The Red Sox were in seventh place in the American League, and I wanted to tell him how great the Yankees were doing, just to piss him off. Too bad they lost to the Dodgers in the 1963 World Series. The fine was about ten bucks. We gave the judge all our loose change.

Back on the road, I saw a turnoff for Omaha. Growing up, I'd heard so many goddamn advertisements for Mutual of Omaha that I figured I might as well check it out. Someone told us the city was named after an Indian tribe. So, when we went into a hardware store (the most interesting spot there) to buy some 3-in-One Oil, I mentioned to the Don Knotts salesman that I lived on Wamsutta Avenue—just to get on an even Native American footing. There wasn't anything else to talk about. On South 42D Street, we hit a pool hall, where we drank piss-warm beer, ate some uncooked hot dogs, and hustled a few locals for gas money (I forgot to mention, I was pool-sharp, having worked at Mr. And Mrs. Cue in Worcester). All in all, Omaha was a godforsaken, lonely place. Loneliness gave me the shakes. I didn't have to be with other people, but I couldn't be around abandoned buildings and zombies. So, we got out of Omaha fast.

When we got to Chicago, we went straight to Northwestern University and stayed in one of the empty women's dormitories. It was our remote tribute to Northwestern alum Ann-Margret. After all, we'd seen a lot of her that summer as Elvis' squeeze. The dorm's beds were comfortable, and it had great vending machines. Not only did they have my favorite cigarette brand (Marlboro filters), but they were filled with enough money to get us back to Massachusetts.

* * *

I was ready to start my senior year at Clark University. Just like that, I went from our hijinks on Landfair to studying shit courses like accounting and marketing. Life was getting serious. The day of reckoning was in sight. The clouds were parting, and, in the sky, I saw a sign that warned: Prepare to Leave Home and Get a Job!

For now, I was still living at 28 Wamsutta, fighting with my mother 24/7. I remember sitting in my car, in the driveway, listening on the radio to JFK giving a speech in Houston. My family loved JFK and having someone who was from Massachusetts in the White House was magic. Everyone I knew loved and respected Jack Kennedy and then he was assassinated. It changed all our lives.

Vietnam was on everyone's mind. Each of the Crazy Eight had received a Selective Service letter when we turned eighteen. My dad warned me about the Army, telling me more than once, "They are a bunch of bastards." And he hardly ever swore. If you were in school, the draft was deferred. So, most of us were staying in college.

Rick the Prick was belatedly hellbent on going to law school. I couldn't believe he wanted to follow in his father's footsteps and join the firm of Seder and Seder, on Main Street. Slobby Robby was working at a liquor store that his father, Irving, bought for him also on Main Street. Ronnie Meenes—aka Meenie Peenie—left his Good Humor truck parked in the garage and went into food catering with his sisters. Dirty Art, who was attending Worcester Junior College, would occasionally help them make submarine sandwiches. That is, when he wasn't working at Olympic Sports, his father's company, putting letters on sports uniforms and assembling trophies. Art was turning into a country boy, spending more time at his family's place in Spencer, swimming in Cranberry Meadow Pond.

Barry Solomon ("Monk") was also supposed to be working for his father as a chemical supplies salesman. That was pure myth. He was traveling around the world—living in his own Monky world. He'd say things like "We just flew here by plane," or "Ask the waitress if we can get some cold ice." He'd introduce himself as "Manfred Klitsch, Global Head of Bazooka Bubble Gum." He'd call us from cities like Munich, saying he was partying on a strip of nightspots called The Raibabone. No one had ever heard of The Raibabone. But Monk seemed to be enjoying himself in this imaginary place every week. He emphatically told me, "You must come to The Raibabone! I just returned from The Raibabone!" Or he was in France, in Cannes on La Croisette, bound for some director's yacht, or in Paris dining at Fouquet's on the Champs-Èlysées. In London, he'd be clubbing on The King's Road. Monk could find the hot spot in Antarctica. When anyone asked me about Monk, I'd say, "The international kid is on the loose."

Then there was Muffin, who'd also been going to Clark. One weird night at a late-night deli, Muffin and I met two Irish guys; their faces and hands were blackened. One was a Dubliner named Mike Murphy; his buddy was called Finn. They were both welders at American Steel and Wire, down the street from Holy Cross College. They were oddly bundled up in thick topcoats and leggings because, as they explained, when you work with industrial cauldrons and ladles full of molten steel all day, it felt freezing when you stepped outside.

After we got to talking, they told us they played blackjack and, coincidentally, so did we. We went back to their flat on the first floor of a dank four-decker. There we drank beer—depositing the empty cans in a waist-high trash basket—and played twenty-one for several days and nights. Neither of the Irish could count. I would deal Mike a picture card—like a nine of spades, or a seven of hearts—and he would say, "Ten plus seven is fourteen, and nine is twenty." Or I'd deal him three picture cards and he would say "I tink I'm a little bit over."

We took them for a couple of hundred bucks. As one can imagine, they got pissed off and told me to keep "fecking" dealing. The trash can was brimming with Pabst Blue Ribbon cans. All four of us were shit-faced. You cannot outdrink an Irishman, especially an immigrant from Ireland. We were doomed to play until the Twelfth of Never. We were prisoners. We couldn't leave that card table except to piss. When Mike and his Buddy finally passed out, we split with whatever we'd won—glad to be the feck out of there.

Joel Robbins—better known as Leoj Snibbor—was my best friend in the C8 and my confidant. Like me, he was studying business at Clark. It wasn't a genuine business school. There was a marketing course that taught us how to read newspaper department store ads. It was less enlightening than my UCLA Development of Jazz class.

Joel and I had an accounting professor named John Hargess, otherwise known as "Harggie Baba." He and my UMass professor Rudolph Kyler were comrades in arms when it came to destroying business college courses. Hargess would scribble accounting theory on the blackboard. As he worked his way down the board, he would inadvertently rub out all his notations with one or more of his stomachs. He would then cluelessly turn to the class, his three-piece pinstripe suit covered in white chalk, to explain what he had erased.

I dreaded the thought of being an accountant—wearing a green visor and crunching numbers. But Joel took accounting seriously. Joel's father was in the home heating oil business, and Joel was slated to take it over.

He was the first one of the Eight to have a serious job and girlfriend—Judy. They married when he was twenty-one and fresh out of Clark.

Meanwhile, in my broken heart, I continued to believe that Linda was in love with me. I wasn't giving up. Golubs don't quit, they just keep embarrassing themselves with illusion and coy women. She always seemed to slide away from me and back to Gordon. I chose to believe that she was being forced into an arranged marriage to a local aristocrat by her hag mother. Her MIT man had her Saran-wrapped so tightly that it was hard for me to penetrate the plastic swaddle. But I did get my licks in. About once or twice a month, I managed to get on her vacillating schedule. We'd go out in Boston and sometimes in Worcester. We were still having sex. She was meeting the standard of most momentary girlfriends. She was apparently guiltless. I never heard the words "I have a boyfriend," or "I'm going steady," or "I have to be faithful"—the usual '60s mantra. Therefore, I condoned her behavior with him.

My friendship with Alan went on unabated. The weekend Boston parties were nonstop. On weeknights, I was sleeping in the same uncomfortable bed I'd occupied since I was 10. But, most weekdays, I was out. My parents hardly ever saw me. I regret it now. I should have spent more time with them. They were young and we could have talked about a lot of family stuff I now know nothing about. But that is the way it works.

My father had been so screwed over in the grocery business—working for pennies. He cared only about feeding the poor people who shopped there. If he didn't have a product, he would tell the customer to wait and he would go around the corner to a chain store and buy it for more than he would sell it. I spent hundreds of hours delivering groceries in the snow and rain, on Saturday and Sunday nights, climbing splintered steps to the top floors of walk-up tenements, where the halls smelled of piss and shit, because my dad had said those poor kids had to eat.

He had no concern for profit. The neighborhood was full of welfare recipients. My dad would cash any check they brought in. A lot of those checks were stolen or forgeries. They would bounce. When I was young, I worked behind the cash register with him and saw him loan money that would never be paid back. He would give away food and allow shoplifters to get away with stolen canned goods.

The store was always short on cash. He would do anything to keep it afloat. For instance, my parents hosted a Tuesday night cha-cha-cha party where an instructor would teach couples the dance that Xavier Cugat had spread across America. I made a point to leave the house on Tuesdays. But you could count on seeing Max and Rose Meenes (no relation to Meenie Peenie). My parents would vacation with them in the Catskills. Max was an overweight, hairless, real estate developer who built some big projects. One cha-cha-cha night, my dad quietly asked Max if he'd mind stopping by his grocery. The following day, Max pulled into the Green Street Market parking lot, in his white Cadillac de Ville. My dad came out in his butcher's apron. I was standing against the wall watching.

Lowering his car's electric window, Max croaked in his raspy voice, "Charlie, why did you want to meet with me?"

He began circling the Caddy around my dad.

My dad confessed, "The store isn't doing well, Max. I wonder if you might be able to make a small loan."

"A *what*?" Max said with a frown that made it clear dad had exceeded the boundaries of a cha-cha-cha lesson.

"Only a few bucks," my father said.

From the sidewalk, I watched that prick circling my father like the Sioux routing Custer. Finally, without saying yes or no, Max drove off, leaving my dad in a cloud of exhaust.

All these degrading moments drove me crazy. The only way to stop feeling sorry for my dad was to make money and make sure my parents were respected in Worcester.

I took advantage of whatever academics Clark had to offer. Clark would be a stepping stone. I would study and get grades good enough to get into law school. It wasn't going to be Harvard or Yale, but it was going to be somewhere—a place where I could get that degree, a means to an end.

* * *

After graduating in 1964, I went to work on Cape Cod, where much of Massachusetts spends its summer vacation. Muffin convinced me to work with him at a seaside resort in New Seabury. I didn't know a thing about being a waiter or a busboy. The guests were paying a fortune for a week on the ocean and most of the kids who served them, like me, were crazy. If one of the diners complained about the chopped liver, the waiter would take the plate back to the kitchen, put the scoops of chopped liver on the floor, jump up and down on them, then scoop them back onto the plate. The guest would usually say, "That's much better!" Muffin, who'd worked at The Concord resort in the Catskills, claimed to know a waiter who jerked off into the re-served food of a complaining customer.

The dining room manager's name was Mr. Silver, but everyone called him "Mr. Shilver." He was an angry man from Sunnyside, Queens. When Muffin introduced me, he told Shilver I was an experienced waiter who had worked with him at The Concord—a pro who could handle the busiest shifts. The hype worked. Shilver hired me, and I was assigned to one of the best tables in the main dining room.

Trying to look like I knew what I was doing, I put on my white ankle-length apron and wrapped a white towel around my waist. Shilver paired me with another kid.

"This is Steve, your lackey," I thought I heard him say.

I immediately started imperiously ordering Steve around: "Steve, get me the maple syrup! Steve, get me the napkins! Steve, set up the coffee pot!"

After a few days of Steve running around like a headless chicken, he said, "Golub, why are you telling me what to do all the fucking time? You're not my boss!"

"Wait a minute," I snapped, "Goddamn, do everything I tell you to do!"

"What are you talking about? Where the hell did you get that?"

"Shilver!" I bellowed back. "He told me you're my lackey,"

"My last name is *Urlaqui*," he explained. "It's French! Get it? Golub, you're a fucking idiot!"

I'd honestly thought summer resorts had lackeys, like medieval courts had vassals. I'd previously checked with Harvey Kaplan, an experienced waiter who'd worked his way through medical school at summer resorts. He disingenuously confirmed that lackeys did work in the dining room.

Harvey was as smooth as cream cheese, a handsome, redhead and a real Don Juan. He had that Alan Golden charisma and all the girls at the hotel were crazy about him. But he was a little crazy and didn't give a shit what people thought. He had a huge, circumcised dick and didn't mind showing it off.

On the first weekend of the summer, he was waiting on a large table of extremely demanding guests in their seventies and eighties. One woman who could have been Harvey's grandmother was grumbling about her tuna salad. With a polite air, Harvey took her plate back to the kitchen. Once there, he took his pants off, returning to the table with his waiter's towel tied around his waist. Carefully centering the tuna salad before the old lady, he stood to the side and asked, "Will that be all, Madam?" As she lifted her fork, she looked up at Harvey who was pretending to be drying his hands with the ends of the towel. Dangling in front of her nose was the longest schlong most people probably had ever seen.

She screamed so loudly, it brought Shilver immediately to the table, who fired Harvey on the spot. Harvey had reached the point of critical mass in the food service business.

A few days after I'd started, I was fired. I couldn't fake it any longer. With my inexperience, I couldn't survive the crossfire between the chefs' demands and the diners' carping. Almost at the same time, Muffin was canned for arguing with the bread boy.

Since I was on the Cape, I went down to Falmouth with Muffin and immediately got a job as a bartender at Jack Banan's Lounge, on Route 28. The place was decorated like a Trinidadian calypso bar; it even had a steel band. Muffin and I rented a small red shingled one-story house around the corner at 195 John Parker Road. There was only one bedroom and a large kitchen/living room. It was a dump but cheap.

I immediately invited my good friend Dave Mason, who'd just graduated from Dartmouth, to stay with us. Dave was a skinny body-builder who wore black horn-rimmed glasses. He drove a cool 1957 black Thunderbird. He and the car looked alike. Dave's father, George Mason, was a low-key guy who had a big law practice in Worcester. For some reason, we started calling Dave "George." He and I got on like a house on fire. We started calling the C8 "The Crazy Eight Plus George." Every one of us liked that new designation.

George, who wore contacts, was hanging out with a hot girl named Twanette. Her sister was the famed dancer Twyla Tharp. Anyone could see, with or without contacts, that Twanette had a body carved out of rock. It was impossible to look at her and not think bad things. One night in July, after a wicked round of bartending, I came home to some unusual circumstances: Twanette was asleep in my bed naked.

It was dark and I didn't know she was there until I climbed under the covers. There she was and ... as kids say today, I was "bricked up." Before I could utter "No, you're my friend's girlfriend," I got swept away in the moment. I'd sworn I would never violate a friend's trust, especially with his girlfriend. But I broke the bro code.

When it was over, she looked at me in a tantalizing way and I said, "Should we do it again?"

"Let's be extravagant" was her answer. We sinned again.

Shortly afterward, George showed up. He sensed something had happened.

"Did you fuck Twanette?" he asked.

Without hesitation I admitted I had. In exchange he immediately punched me in the face. I retaliated by putting him in a headlock, then running him across the room and smashing his head through a windowpane. Twanette did nothing to stop us. The slugfest seemed to last for hours. Finally, Muffin poked a garden hose through a window and drenched us both. The fight wound down. George and I stood in opposite corners glaring at one another. The house was destroyed. A few hours later, George split. Regrettably, I don't think I ever saw him again.

In the afternoons I worked as a chauffeur for Mrs. Norman Dupee. She was an elegant, extremely nice woman in her eighties. Her family had a compound in Falmouth—that is, several large houses in a secluded area owned exclusively by the Dupees. Rich people on the Cape, like the Kennedys, liked compounds.

I wore a black uniform. Every afternoon, after filling her thermos with warm milk, I would drive Mrs. Dupee in her black four-door 1956 Cadillac to the beach. We never left the car. She and I would watch the sea gulls and waves from 3 to 4 p.m. and talk about everything under the sun. She was particularly intrigued about what went on at Jack Banan's. She even visited me there once, at 11 p.m. on a Saturday. God only knows what she was doing up at that hour. I served her a Singapore Sling. Every Wednesday afternoon she hosted a cocktail party for her three best lady friends. I would bartend, making strong martinis as they requested. They sat, slightly bombed, stiff as socialites, at a round bridge table, gossiping about Cape Cod and Boston Brahmin life.

One of those afternoons, as I was jiggling the gin and vermouth, her sterling silver bullet-shaped cocktail shaker slipped from my grasp. It flew across the room—rocketing past Mrs. Dupee and her friends, and crashing into the brick fireplace. That livened up the gathering.

"Oh my!" Mrs. Dupee remarked. "Richard, I thought you mixed cocktails at that calypso bar?"

"Yes, Ma'am," I replied. "But mostly beer and wine."

Working for Mrs. Dupee was the high point of that summer. She considered me family. We kept in touch until she passed away a few years later.

CHAPTER 15:

St. Paul is a Street Not an Apostle

By the end of August, I had been accepted to law school at Temple University, in Philadelphia, and the University of North Carolina, in Chapel Hill. I was still anxiously waiting to hear from Boston University, my first choice. But, by now, I'd come to accept that dreams rarely get fulfilled.

Then, unexpectedly, a different acceptance arrived from Bean Town. Linda called me. She'd been on a second trip to another slice of Europe and had returned to start her third year at Boston University. She said she was excited about the coming school year. As always, she was proud to tell me she was in the School of Fine and Applied Arts and, to boot, one of its star students. (She never mentioned that our mutual friend, Deeny Yudell, had gotten into Yale Art School.) She asked if I would come to Boston. My mother was flabbergasted but pleased; she still liked Linda. So, in the early morning, I raced up Route 9 and got to her dormitory, on Bay State Road, around noon.

Man, I was excited. I was glad that I didn't fall for Donna Kling or go out with Tina Louise. I was more comfortable around Linda. Still, in the back of my mind I feared this visit would be apocalyptic. Wasn't she crazy about Gordon? Wasn't everything good happening to them in their relationship and all things bad were pushing me further into the down-swing, the nadir of romance? Beware, I unconvincingly told myself, we are right at the beginning of life and that's a long road, so relax, just play it out, the pendulum of fate will swing the right way.

There she was, skipping down the steps to meet me. That was a stark cold physical reality. She looked radiant; she even had a mild tan that matched her brown eyes. I'd never seen her in any skin color other than milk pale white. We were in the flow that day. We aimlessly walked around Beacon Street holding hands, no destination in mind, occasionally kissing. Fantasies were coming true. I was twenty-one years old. It was September, the leaves were turning early, the light was a brilliant amber. This was that moment in time and there would not be another. As the afternoon wore on, we became closer and closer. There was a harmony that I'd never felt before. I was reaching the Massachusetts version of Nirvana. Olympus. No question, she felt it, too.

I rightfully started to think that today was our day—this was the moment I would propose to her. The weight of the past was lifting. As the sun slipped down behind the Charles River, I became more convinced that this time it was right. Over a romantic dinner, she told me that she was leaving her dorm, that she'd signed a lease on an apartment, a fourth-floor walk-up on St. Paul Street. She wanted me to see it, maybe we'd live there. In her eyes I could see much more. I brought up the subject of marriage. Things were going so well it seemed like this was the perfect moment. I wasn't nervous. Her reaction was positive. She said she'd always loved me. She didn't say yes, but she said she would seriously think about it.

On the walk to her apartment she asked, "Can I paint your portrait? Would you pose for me? Would you take your clothes off?"

It was a strange turn. I became suspicious. Had the whole day been leading just to this? Was I just an artist's model? The complexion of the day was changing as it got dark.

We were now in the apartment, a small gray living room, a gray carpet where she'd placed a small couch and an armchair. We talked for a while about the portrait—my self-consciousness emerged. My weakness was apparent. The mood was changing. It was after midnight. I felt paralyzed until she took my hand and guided me toward another dimension. She led me into another gray room. The bedroom. Her mother's condescension, the country club, her brother's hostility—all of those were instantly things of the so-distant past. Now it was just the two of us in her boudoir, miles beyond the pink room, in a real city, with my proposition of marriage floating in the air. Finally, a real bond was forming.

It didn't take us long to get into bed and begin going at each other furiously. She was the more aggressive one. The silk underwear she'd purchased in Paris was soon on the floor and I was deep inside her. Her breathing was thick, intense. She was sweating, biting my ear, right on the verge of orgasm when … the doorbell rang.

"Who the hell could that be?" I asked. "How can anyone know you're here?"

Instantly, the romance was a fucking joke.

"It's Michael," the satirist said to the pessimist. "I told him I'd be here."

She was totally untroubled by the pernicious situation she'd created. Her perspiration seemed to disappear. Her milky white complexion was back. She was herself again. I was in agony, my stomach folded in half. Before I could comprehend the situation, she was out of bed and changing into her white lace nightgown.

"Where are you going?" I insisted.

"He's downstairs. I'm going to see him." There was no tone in that voice other than determination.

She was out the door. The bitch was going on a night flight. I went out to the stairwell landing, and in my skin, peered over the railing, and watched her walk down four winding flights to the lobby where Gordon was standing. Waiting. This was Kensington Road revisited—the time when she was with me and he pulled up in his red Corvette, taking her away for ice cream. Only this time it was Linda-induced coitus interruptus.

They spoke for over twenty minutes while I stood and squirmed with indignation. Then she walked up to the apartment, where I sat undressed in the armchair—destroyed by her duplicity.

She entered and, without hesitation, said, "I could've invited him up, but *you* were here."

"You?" This was sheer mockery. It sounded like I was a kitchen water bug that was about to be crushed.

Standing there in the nude, I felt extremely vulnerable, even weak, but I gathered myself together and contained my anger. Women have suffered much more than an argument for the mere scent of infidelity. The room stank of what I thought she was intending.

"I want you to leave," she commanded as if I'd never been there. "Please go back to Worcester!" Her voice was telling and firm.

"Leave, so you can invite him up and fuck him? No way! I'm staying right here and, if I drive back to Worcester, you're coming with me."

The argument seesawed for about an hour. At around 2 a.m., both of us had enough. She finally relented, saying she'd go back to Worcester with me, my insurance that she wouldn't be flat on her back, under Gordon, in the gray bedroom. By this time Gordon must have been asleep.

Driving back, she wept inexorably through Brookline, Natick, Framingham, Westborough, and Shrewsbury, finally drying out as we reached Lake Quinsigamond. I think the sight of water overwhelmed her tears. The faucets were finally cranked off. Between sobs she repeated, "It's over between us. It can't work. I can't see you again." Keeping my eyes on the road, I argued to the contrary, to no avail.

It was about 4 a.m. when we reached her house on Kensington. I pulled in the driveway, and we were once again sitting in the dark in the same spot. It would be the last time and we were a long way from me jumping in the straw and that dumb fucking invitation from Steve Krintzman.

"Are you sure it's over?" I pitched one more time. "Are you certain?"

Then she turned, looked me straight in the eye, and said, "No, I'm not sure about anything. Please call me this morning at 8."

It felt like another staple in my fingernail. But being that a sucker is born every day, I said I would call.

She walked to the back door, peered at me, and went inside.

I went home and stayed up the rest of the morning, psychotically waiting for 8 A.M.

When the time came, I called her number: SWift 11069. It rang three times, four times, five times. There was no answer. The pendulum moved beyond my grasp.

I was immeasurably angry. I decided I wasn't going to wait to hear from BU. My resolve was to head to North Carolina. I awakened my mother and asked her to help me pack. That must have been painful for her and my dad but when you're twenty-one, one doesn't have the depth to understand how heartbreaking it is to see a child move away from home. Brewster Academy had been close by in New Hampshire, but North Carolina was another story.

I packed everything I could into my car—including my dog, Pike, a black-and-white Siberian husky. He was sitting in the back seat on a pile of sweatshirts—ready to go. Somehow Pike knew more about Linda than I did. He knew she wasn't going to call.

Pike and I said goodbye to my parents. My mother was helpful and sympathetic; after all, this was clearly a material crossroad. On the grueling trip down to Chapel Hill, I stopped for a few days in Wilmington,

Delaware, staying with my uncle, William Brodie. Bill was like a father to me but could talk to me in a way my father couldn't. I recounted my tale of woe from beginning to end, feeling the weight of each word retroactively. I wept on one of his shoulders, then the other. He was deeply understanding, and he told me I needed to focus on the future, not a broken relationship.

I went into the bathroom and looked in the mirror and was stunned by the reflection. My face had taken on the features of my father. He was me and I was him. In that moment, I knew I had a binding link with all the Golubs who had come before me—an unmistakable genetic lineage that I was not going to compromise for a woman who didn't care for me. I was determined to move that link forward. After I left Uncle Bill's, I felt stronger, or at least ready for the labor of law school. I was in no substantive way over her. But I knew it was finished and would never be rekindled. The end has an unmistakable thud. I had hit bottom. What was left was my impenetrable pride. She couldn't get through that layer. No one could.

Late that afternoon, I reached Washington, D.C. I recalled my dream to be a page boy and, for the hell of it, drove past Congress. I parked and took Pike for a walk on the grass. It was a fake-nostalgia walk in which I imagined that I had once worked as a Capitol page. I thought about calling my irascible Uncle Rube, my mother's brother who lived nearby, but I didn't. One uncle was enough to fulfill my grieving needs. I stared at the Capitol and thought about all the bad laws that had been passed inside that building. There was no time to waste. I wanted to get on with the business of law school. It was so damn ironic: Alan had gotten into law school at Boston University, even after we'd broken laws in Massachusetts, Texas, Nevada, Nebraska, and California. There were no laws in Juarez. You can't fully understand a rule until you break it. So, I had some background before I got into the curriculum.

Chapel Hill looked like a classic college town, not anything like Wolfeboro, New Hampshire. It was a bucolic enclave, lined with every kind of tree and flower that grows in the South—from bald cypress to red azaleas. Most of the residents never left, declaring themselves to be true-blue Carolinians. Their world of entertainment consisted of Carolina basketball, football, and baseball. They also seemed to be constantly talking about how much they disliked Duke University. That was, as they were on their way to a golf course in their banana-colored outfits. It wasn't as friendly as Mrs. Dupee's Cape Cod compound.

Although it wasn't the deep South, Chapel Hill was cavernous with racial prejudice masked by the preppie outfits that clothed the student body. It smacked me in the head, as I drove down East Franklin Street, the town's main thoroughfare, passing the Robert E. Lee Bar. There wasn't a Black person anywhere near that tavern then or later, when I checked it for drinking purposes. I confirmed that Blacks were not welcome in the General's drinking haunt, nor at countless other places in this quaint village. Most Black residents lived nearby in East Carrboro.

I parked and walked, with Pike, around campus. On fraternity row, I saw the Delta Kappa Epsilon house. It was a brick, neoclassical mansion, with tall columns. The DKE door was wide open, so I walked right in. A few of the athletic-looking brothers were on a couch drinking. I told them I was here to attend UNC law school and asked if they had room for me and Pike to stay for a few days.

"No problem, Yankee," one of the brothers drawled.

They liked my style and loved Pike even more. So that closed the deal.

I moved into a second-floor room decorated with beat-up road signs, a yellow fire hydrant, pennants, and a large Confederate flag.

I'd parked my car nearby, in front of a small free-standing real estate office, on East Franklin Street. After a day or two, I ambled into the office. The receptionist/broker, Shirley Lloyd, told me about a new Valley Park rental complex up the road toward Durham. Shirley said she herself lived there. We talked for a while. I learned that she was twenty-five and had moved from Richmond, Virginia. Eventually, she said that, if I wanted to get out of the DKE house, I was welcome to stay with her while I was getting my bearings. Considering that she was tall and attractive and wore her brunette hair in a French twist, it was a damn good invitation that I couldn't turn down. Her hospitality came at the right time during my lamentation. I moved in.

The location of Shirley's unit—directly opposite a sewage treatment plant with a sweeping armature that incessantly sprayed chemicals—interfered with my romantic inclinations. But, after tightly shutting all the windows, the place was livable. After a couple of fling nights with Shirley, I could see she was falling for me. But Linda was still weighing heavily on my mind. I wasn't ready for another relationship. So, Shirley introduced me to a neighbor who had an extra room.

Charles Bluhm was a tall, thin, good-looking guy a little older than me. "Charlie Boy" was a Latin scholar and taught first-year classics at the university. Hailing from Jacksonville, Florida, he was full of genuine "I wish I was in Dixie" charm. He named his dog The Colonel and at least once a day Charles would tell me, "That damn dog can't hunt worth a shit." But The Colonel bonded with Pike, and Charles and I did, too. We were off to the races.

Charles wore blue Brooks Brothers shirts and belted khaki pants. There were no other outfits. He'd call Brooks Brothers and say, "This here is Charlie Bluhm, send me some blue shirts." The store knew his family, the shirts would arrive neatly bundled a day or two later. Charles was divorced, as were his parents, as were his two younger brothers, who'd each been married twice. That came to six divorces. (If they had the same lawyer, they could've negotiated a group discount.) Now, Charles was living with a German blond named Scottie Troxler. Early on, Charles informed me that Scottie was a find because (a) she accepted his idiosyncrasies, (b) she sometimes looked like a woman and at other times like a man, and (c) she could passionately, in her efficient Teutonic way, suck his testicle.

Charles had just one. He was born that way. "It didn't bother me, Richie," he would say.

Charles was a drinker, but he miraculously got up at 7 each morning. Some alcoholics can do that. He'd scramble some eggs and onions, hide his bloodshot eyes behind green-lensed Ray-Bans, mount his blue-and-white 250 cc NSU motorcycle, revving it to the max, and remark, "Richard, goddamnit, the day has to have an ascendancy and here we go! I'm off to teach my class!" Often, I'd jump on the back, and he'd drop me at Manning Hall, the law building.

On one of those school mornings, he argued fiercely with Scottie. At one end of the living room, she stood stark naked and threw an empty Bacardi bottle at him. Then he hurled a fresh rib-eye steak at her. The well-marbled beef coiled around her forehead. It was quite a look.

"Charles, you wouldn't try to hurt me if you loved me," she insisted. "Don't you love me?"

"Scottie, this is how I feel about you," he replied. "If I saw your automobile across the street, I wouldn't make any more of an effort to let the air out of the tires than I would to pump them up."

Their relationship ended shortly before Christmas, and I never saw Scottie again. That termination gave me a deeper perspective on relationships.

Charles regularly invited the Classics Department to our apartment, where the faculty would chat exclusively in Latin. They'd often quote the raunchy rhymes of Catullus. Charles' motivation to teach was partly driven by his close friendship with the department head, Al Suskind, whose beautiful, raven-haired wife, Lavinia, a Duchess of Alba dream, was Charles' paramour. In his way, Charles loved both Al and Lavinia.

As soon as his classes were finished, usually by noon, Charlie Boy would be back home on his bender. He drank Bacardi black rum and soda on the rocks. At least one full quart a day was about his limit or until he passed out. Quite often when he was knocking the rum back, Charles would lapse into telling me how smart he was.

"You know, Richie, I am one brilliant motherfucker," he'd say. "I'm a member of Mensa with an IQ of 150. Do you know that on the Stanford-Binet test I scored in the 99th percentile? That means that out of 100 people I'm smarter than 99. Open the damn Merriam-Webster dictionary, pick out any word. I'll tell you the definition. Or open the Almanac and ask me any question."

For starters, I asked him how many submarines the Russian Navy had in 1964 and he answered, correctly, 424.

It was a set piece.

His mind was encyclopedic. He was the smartest person I ever met. I often wondered if our meeting was really happenstance. Was he purposely there to show me another side of life? In a way, it wasn't different from meeting Linda on that ill-fated hayride—a road that could not have been averted. Charlie was meant to help me talk through my emotions. It took a ton of Bacardi and lots of late nights, but his classical education put Linda in perspective. He informed me that it was way too early to figure out the drama's denouement. In Greek plays, things don't work themselves out until a long period of time elapses.

"Aristotle is my teacher," he said. "Linda just might come back around, just you wait and see, Richie. Don't be a dumb shit. Consult Aristotle! Do you understand *anagnorisis*? Things may go from bad to good. Your fortunes may be reversed. Michael Gordon and Linda have been putting you through the opposite route, *peripeteia*. But the plot can change. Man, you are stuck in a fucking Greek tragedy."

Coincidentally, in the auditorium on opening day, the dean, Dixon Philips, a sophisticated, small man with a kind heart, gave a rousing speech to the first-year class, admonishing us, "There are two ways to go through law school. One is with a bludgeon, the other with a rapier." Not much different from what Charlie said. It was advice that a good deal of the class didn't heed; over 60 percent flunked out the first year.

Most of the students were from North Carolina and a high percentage were NC State grads. The class of 150 had three women. Being from Massachusetts separated me from the Southern good old boys, of which there was a never-ending supply. There were plenty of hicks in Massachusetts but no hillbillies in Worcester. Once during a coffee break in our contracts class, one of them threateningly whispered to me, "I ain't never seen a Jew before."

There were four Jewish guys in the class. The other three were from New York. They were, as my mother would say, "schleppers." (Yiddish for hangers-on.) I had no interest in hanging with them. Instead, I befriended a blond wild man named Terence Hoffmann. He was from Syracuse, New York. He had two brothers and six sisters, one of whom, Susan Hoffmann, later became internationally known as Viva, the Andy Warhol superstar.

Terry didn't give a damn about law school. He was a natural performer. In torts class, in front of 100 students, he jumped on his desk and stood there until he had everyone's attention. Then he acted out all the parts of Act I of *Billy Budd*. At the end of the first semester, I found Terry's beat-up contracts book under a desk. It appeared he'd never opened it, never studied a sentence. He flunked out at the end of the first year.

Outside of Terry I didn't really have any friends except Charlie. He would regale me with captivating stories. His alcoholic, peg-leg father, the former mayor of Jacksonville, was now dating the town tramp and living in a huge house that overlooked the Intracoastal Waterway. Oceangoing vessels would cruise past the floor-to-ceiling picture windows of his father's home, seeming like they were going to dock in his living room, while dad was lying on the floor, walnut leg up in the air, in full view, getting a blow job.

In November, during a weeknight when we were partying hard, I received a call from Muffin.

"Hello, Itsy! It's me, Dworkin."

Muffin, now at Ohio State, had paid me a few visits in Chapel Hill. Charles called him Eddie Duhvorzhaak after the composer Antonin Dvorak. He thought Muffin was odd and often fondly asked about Duhvorzhaak, although he would say from time to time, "I don't understand that guy."

"What's going on?" I asked Muffin. "I'm in the middle of a party and I'm with a beautiful woman. You're interrupting me."

I was annoyed because he'd interrupted my momentum with Judy Dudley, a real campus queen, whom I wanted to get to know in my room.

"You should know," Muffin said, "Linda got engaged to Michael Gordon."

"I should what?" I asked, my lips together. "Isn't it predictable? You always go out of your way to give me bad news."

I hung up. It ruined the night and the rest of the week.

I threw myself deeply into law school. The European system is primarily based on written laws. The American law school education is based on studying what happened in cases that were full of facts, too many facts. There was a shitload of memorization. I was having a hard time separating the real law from judicial opinions, which were largely incomprehensible and subjective. These opinions were often written by stupid judges, many of whom were elected.

The stress of law was starting to affect me physically—just as geometry had at Worcester Academy. Worried about me again, my dad called Dean Philips and told him that I was going through hell. But I forged my way through the academic morass. Toward the end of the first semester, I began to see the light.

I spent most nights studying at Manning Hall's law library. One night, around 10, one of the students from New York yelled, "Hey Golub, get over here. Look out the window!"

On the Manning front lawn were four Ku Klux Klansmen in purple silk robes and matching pointed hoods—marching across campus carrying fiery torches and a 15-foot burning wooden cross. Nothing in life scared me more than that—not even that rumble the Crazy Eight had with the Tatnuck Boys at Newton Square. The next weekend, a thousand Klansmen, clad in white robes with red stripes, marched down West Main Street in Durham, brandishing oversize steel flashlights in broad daylight. Marching with them were women and children.

This wasn't exactly the best place for a New England Jew boy. But I wasn't leaving. No one seemed to be conscious of the passage of the 1964 Civil Rights Act. It was never mentioned during my three years at law school. It puzzled me that there were many smart guys in my class who really knew the law but never discussed race—apart from two classmates I overheard talking about "stringing up" a Black student they'd seen talking to a white girl.

More than ever, I wanted to make my father—who'd fought the Nazis—proud of me. I wanted nothing more than to finish law school, start practicing, and free my family from the stigma of the grocery business. The Golub name had to be respected.

* * *

In June of 1965, I'd survived the first year of law school. Pike and I returned to Worcester. I had no plans for the summer. Ambling down Shrewsbury Street, I looked up at the egg-shaped, white metal sign for BUTLER CHEVROLET, which at night was illuminated by over 100 rotating marquee lights. Planted at the edge of the used car lot, the sign stood fifty feet high. I stepped inside the new-car showroom. I instantly recognized Gordon

Butler, whose Lebanese family had dealerships here and in Providence. He had just unsuccessfully run for Congress in Rhode Island. He was sitting behind a salesman's desk that seemed too small for him.

The room was swimming with brand new 1965 Chevrolets of all colors and models. Not my favorite car. When driven over 20 mph, Chevys drifted all over the road. Nevertheless, I was there to be a hypocrite, to sell out, like everyone else in this world who sold something. I walked over and introduced myself. He was an impressive figure, tall, handsome, and imperious. His swarthy skin gave him an air of mystery. I'd seen photos of him on his sailboat, *The Nomad*, with his girlfriend, Patty Paulson, the face of American Airlines. He had it all.

"Mr. Butler," I said, "I just finished my first year of law school at the University of North Carolina. Do you have any summer job openings?"

"Really?" he said. "I went to law school. Tell me about Pierson against Post. In one word."

It was a New York Supreme Court case. In 1802, Pierson had killed a fox in Southampton, New York, when it was being chased by Post. Who had legal possession of the dead fox? But I couldn't recall the facts quickly enough.

"Possession, man," he said with a self-satisfied grin. "Possession."

I shook my head, pissed that he was there with the answer before me.

He hired me anyway. That's what playboys do. Soon afterward, I started selling used cars with lifetime salesmen who dwelled in a little shingled house in the middle of the lot. It became my second home.

The salesmen all wore white shirts with their sleeves rolled up to the elbows. They had tans on their forearms, face, and neck. It was called a "used car salesman tan." Most days there were no customers until midaft-ernoon because everyone in Worcester was working. During the day we'd play cards and shoot dice against the wall of the little house. Even the boss Billy Nyman, would join in because there was nothing to do until you got an "up." That meant it was your turn if a customer walked on the lot. Otherwise, you'd have three or four salesmen charging at the customer, whom they referred to as "the stiff."

Selling used cars was not a science. Once the customer said he was interested in a car and wanted to buy it for the stated price, he would be taken into the little house to sign the contract. Just as the customer was reviewing the papers, a Butler manager would burst into the shack and ask the salesman what price he'd quoted. The salesman would repeat the price. The manager would yell and scream at the salesman, telling him he was "fired" because he sold the car too cheaply. The salesman would pack up and leave. The customer would ask the manager what the real price was and express concern that his new friend, the salesman, had been fired. The manager would then raise the price 10 percent or more. That was called bushwhacking.

It didn't end there. Butler Chevrolet customers had no money. So, if a car were sold, we had to get the customer financed. It meant getting the bank to make a car loan. The bank wouldn't do that unless there was a down payment. So, we had to take the customer to a finance company, like Beneficial Finance or Household Finance, to help them pony up the down payment. There were two steps: first, the finance company, then the bank. That was called "the double dip."

After the car was sold, the customer was escorted into an office, at the new car showroom, for further bushwhacking. The manager told the customer that, sadly, the paint on the car would not last long. Fortunately, Butler had a unique process called Lustre Seal that ensured the paint job would gleam for the life of the car. On the left side of the manager's desk were five drawers with certificates for five Lustre Seal packages. After the customer had chosen one, the manager explained that the warranty on parts and service for the customer's car was limited to three months. Again, fortunately, Butler offered other warranty certificates—contained in the five drawers to the right, each one had a higher price for the same service.

The double-gouged stiff had now bought a car he couldn't afford. He would happily drive the automobile around for a few months. Then it would be repossessed. Butler Chevrolet kept the full sales price.

If a customer voluntarily drove onto the lot, his car was history. A salesman would swoop in and say, "Sir, your car is incredible! Mrs. Winowski, on Grafton Street, is looking for that exact car." The prospective customer's car was soon on its way to Mrs. Winowski. The customer would be forced to buy a used car because he had no way home. Of course, there was no Mrs. Winowski. The car was driven across the street to a garage that had a large canvas flap for a door.

On my first day on the job, I was almost killed. I was "up." My first customer seemed like a nice man—in his thirties, interested in a blue, two-door 1960 Pontiac. He told me all about his job working at a local factory and his family, and asked me technical questions that I had to have answered by my manager, Billy Nyman. Then he asked if he could drive it before he made an offer. I was told that every car had to be test-driven. So, we went for a ride. After I got into the passenger seat, I noticed that the customer had a weird twitch. As we were cruising down Shrewsbury Street, he floored the pedal, pushing the speedometer to 90 miles an hour in thick traffic where the speed limit was 25. I grabbed the wheel and told him to slow down

"You asked me to test drive it and that's what I'm doing, doing," he yelled.

I had him pull over. Sitting in the car, he just stared into space. I drove the car back to the lot. There he seemed to calm down. He asked to see the engine. Looking under the hood, he began to scream, "Valves, pistons! Valves, pistons! Valves, pistons!"

It turned out he was a patient at Worcester State Hospital, across the street. No one had warned me that patients regularly wandered onto the lot and tried to purchase cars. The dealership should have been called Nutler Chevrolet.

Whatever crazy, shady shit Alan or I or the Crazy Eight had pulled, it didn't compare to what went on at Butler. At night, George Butler would visit the used car lot and make all the salesmen line up in front of him. Then he'd unzip his fly, take out his dick, and piss on the base of the flashing BUTLER CHEVROLET sign.

"That sign is fabulous!" he'd bellow in his unmistakable nasal tone. "I'm Mr. Butler! I'm fabulous and I designed that sign! Call me Mr. But-ler!"

At one point in the summer, the Butler family took a vacation in the South of France. Where else? Billy Nyman and the rest of the used car salesmen cleared the lot of cars—except for used Corvettes. Each of us picked out one. Then we drag-raced back and forth in the lot. We did that for three weeks. We sold no cars. When George Butler returned from France, he promptly fired all of us, other than Billy. He made Billy wash cars for a week. Then he fired him.

* * *

I hadn't been in touch with Linda for over a year since that infamous night on St. Paul Street. Late one afternoon, I was on my way back from the golf course, driving down May Street. The light was dusky but, in the car approaching in the oncoming lane, I saw Linda. We locked eyes. Neither of us attempted to stop. We happened to be passing the Temple Emanuel. Little did I know that, in two hours, she would wed inside.

That night, I went to Cambridge to go out with a damn good-looking girl from Holland, whom I'd met at Alan's apartment. She went to school in Bean Town and her family had plenty of beans. She lived off campus, in an old Victorian House on Pearl Street, in sort of a remote area in Cambridge. We went out for dinner, stayed up very late, and we spent the night together at her place.

In the morning, we got up, got dressed, drank coffee. I walked out on her porch. As I stretched and yawned, I heard someone screaming,

"Richard, Richard, Richard!!!"

I looked down at the street. There was a couple in a new tan Volkswagen convertible that had beer cans tied to its bumper. On the car's trunk was a large, crudely crafted sign that proclaimed, "JUST MARRIED."

One of the people was Linda Paul and the other was Michael Gordon.

She was screaming my name over and over.

It was otherworldly—the most unexpected thing of my life. There was no way they could have known I was in Cambridge, forty-three miles from Worcester, much less on obscure Pearl Street.

Minutes later, I was driving behind them. I couldn't help it. To me, Linda seemed to be crying for help. She was turned around on her knees, looking straight at me and waving furiously, as if to say, "Rescue me!"

A minute later we were on Massachusetts Avenue, headed in the direction of Boston. She was still frantically waving at me when Gordon grabbed her around the neck and belligerently pulled her over to him. When we arrived at Storrow Drive, the crosstown parkway that wraps around the Charles River, they turned to the right. I took a left.

The next time I saw Linda was twenty-seven years later. She called me.

EPILOGUE

When you are crazy enough to write a memoir in your late seventies, it's an endurance contest. Can I get this done? Memories are painfully elusive. I sought out people I knew, and didn't know, as fact-checkers but many of them turned out to be dead. So many impressions are subjective, but the facts are the facts. The past is a cheetah. It moves quickly and then it disappears. What happened to these characters one knew? What was their purpose? It's human to search for meaning, but is there any?

There wasn't a week that went by, when I was growing up, that I didn't have a snapshot of where I'd be when I was older. I was in my forties, standing by myself in a black suit, with the horizon in the background. It looked like I'd done okay. If Linda had only said yes, she would have been in the photo. But I came to see she didn't belong there.

Twenty-seven years after that disastrous night on St. Paul Street, Linda was in the middle of a hotly contested Massachusetts divorce from Michael Gordon. It was 1991. My mother happened to sit next to her at a wedding. Linda confided that she was lonely and she'd been thinking about me. She asked my mother for my number. Late one night, she called me. We planned to meet for lunch in Ayer, Connecticut, halfway between Worcester and New York City, where I now live and practice law.

That day, I drove my steel blue Porsche 911 and wore a pair of Levi's and a white T-shirt. I was vain. I may have been a forty-nine-year-old lawyer, but I worked out and took care of myself. Plus, everyone in my family looked unjustifiably young. On the way, I bought a package of condoms, planning that we would end up at a local motel.

Arriving at our rendezvous, I found that the restaurant was brimming with old folks with walkers and wheelchairs—gratuitously manifesting the passage of time. Linda showed up late in a small, unwashed, older SUV that was loaded with dirty laundry. She wore a wrinkled blue-and-white cotton dress which could have used some dry-cleaning. It was immediately apparent we weren't the same kids.

We sat in a corner. Linda ordered a Kahlua, a geezer drink. I told her that I'd heard from her aunt that Linda and her mother, Helen, had once been in New York City, walking up Fifth Avenue, when Helen ironically said, "Why don't we visit Richard Golub? We're right near his office. I hear he's now a successful lawyer." They never rang my buzzer.

Linda confirmed the story. The conversation quickly shifted from our old emotions to her bitterly contested divorce that lasted for years. It became a legal consultation. I should've whipped out a yellow legal pad and taken notes. She said her marriage had been unhappy from Day One. Shortly after they bought a house in Wayland, Massachusetts, she said, he began to treat her like a handyman, expecting her to perform repairs and landscaping. He even rented a Bobcat excavator and ordered her to level a huge knoll behind their home. She asked me what I knew about Stanley garage door openers.

She told me about a women's self-defense group she'd joined in Boston, because she was fearful of getting raped. She organized a feminist group that met at her house in Wayland. She said that she'd grown afraid of Gordon and that, over the years, he'd come to despise her. She claimed that once, when they were scuba diving, he tried to disconnect her air supply.

Michael's sister, Sandy Hersh, vigorously denied that tale when I relayed it to her. She couldn't even recall Linda ever scuba diving. Sandy did recall that, on a trip in Morocco, Linda became gravely ill, and Gordon was reluctant to get her medical assistance. According to Sandy, he told Linda that, if it weren't for their children, he'd have left her years before. Gordon later married a Mexican woman. After battling dementia, he died in Guadalajara, Mexico, in 2020.

By the end of our lunch, it was clear that Linda had realized she'd picked the wrong guy and that she wanted to get back together with me. But it was too late.

Every six months or so, I'd call her. Our conversations were warm and considerate. We met a few more times. In 2000, I was at a book-signing in Worcester for my legal thriller, *The Big Cut*. During the reading, I looked up and saw her in the front row. I sensed her loneliness and despair. But there was nothing I could do, or wanted to do.

About twenty years ago she told me she had Parkinson's disease. Joel Robbins, my best friend from the Crazy Eight, was also stricken with Parkinson's, as was my good friend Richard Lenett.

They started out in life in Worcester.

Linda, Joel, and Richard spoke from time to time, sharing information about treatments and trying to help one another endure the wicked illness that inevitably claimed all three of their lives.

The loss of a first love casts a long shadow. Never underestimate your experiences when you were too young to comprehend what occurred. You will never stop thinking about them.

* * *

In the summer of 1967, Alan and I began to prepare for the Massachusetts bar exam. We signed up for the PLI bar review course but usually found ourselves hanging out with friends on the North Shore of Boston or playing football. I got injured in one of our scrimmages—which meant I had to spend weeks in bed at 69 Charles Street (with an interesting girl who nursed me back to health). The two-day bar exam consisted of morning and afternoon sessions at Boston College, each three hours. Alan and I arrived at the BC auditorium. He came dressed as Zorro—a character he'd favored since childhood—in black boots, hat, and cape. He marched to his assigned seat and remained standing while he scribbled swashbuckling lines across the exam booklet, as though his pencil were a rapier. He "finished" the first three-hour session in ten minutes, then strutted out the door. He did this for all four sessions. By the second day, the 300 other students, who were initially dumbfounded, got the joke and laughed.

Alan and I both flunked the exam. We fell out of touch until 1971. At that time, I was living in New York's West Village when he called to say he was in the neighborhood. He asked if he could come over with some friends. He showed up with three other guys, all dressed identically in white T-shirts, white shoes, and white pants. That afternoon, Alan told me that he was gay. He also said that he'd been in love with me and that he wanted to finally tell me. I was stunned. In retrospect, thinking about the women he'd ignored on our cross-country trip, it made sense. I told him, as sensitively as possible, that the feeling wasn't mutual, and that I considered him a great friend. By today's standards, I'm sure I'll be criticized for not jumping into bed with him and for not kissing him on the lips.

His friends said they were going to visit the Guggenheim Museum and asked me to join them. We were walking up the Guggenheim's spiral ramp when, on the third floor, Alan climbed the slick white railing and tried to jump. It was a miracle that we were able to pull him down. Sitting on the floor, he tearfully told me he wanted to commit suicide.

During the writing of this memoir, his sister, Arlene, informed me that Alan died of AIDS in 1991. She said he'd struggled with his sexuality but finally embraced it, eventually moving to San Francisco. Unbeknown to me, he'd had two nervous breakdowns during law school and had attempted suicide before. Another example of how, no matter how close you are to someone, you never fully know what's going on inside.

* * *

Linda's brother, Richard Paul, also went to law school but was never admitted to the Massachusetts bar. While playing cards with him during a visit to Worcester, in later years, I misdealt a card, prompting him to call me, once again, "fucking stupid." I snapped, "I'm a practicing lawyer in New York and you flunked the bar three times. Who's stupid?" His face turned red. I never saw him again. He wound up teaching in a Catholic high school for over thirty-nine years. Much to his parents' disappointment, he married a non-Jewish woman. He died at sixty-nine in 2010. According to his obit, he was "a loyal fan of the New England Patriots" and had "an avid interest in Conservative politics."

Richie Lariviere, my co-conspirator in the Worcester Academy cherry-bombing, is alive at this writing. In 2007, he was sentenced to several years in prison for the attempted murder of his wife, Nicki. Other charges included murder-for-hire and arson-for-hire. Described in court as " a man of considerable wealth," he was ordered to pay Nicki $3.6 million, plus interest. Nicki died of cancer six months after Richie's trial …

The Crazy Eight has six survivors, all of whom are doing well. We stay in touch, on a much more regular basis, since losing Joel in 2015 and Ronnie Meenes in 2020. We are planning a reunion in Las Vegas.

Eddie ("Muffin") Dworkin received his Ph.D. in the '60s. He had a private psychological consulting practice for over thirty years in Columbia, Maryland. He recently retired to travel the world and that doesn't include Worcester.

Ricky Seder ("Rick the Prick") is still in Worcester, having retired from the trucking business after successfully practicing law. His personality sparkles with unusual facts. An ardent fisherman, he travels to places like Tierra del Fuego.

"Slobby Robby" still runs Kirsch Liquors on Main Street in Worcester. His customers often leave the store with small, brown paper bags containing an open can of Bud, thus avoiding the open container law. His marriage, to a wealthy woman, didn't end well. But now he has a girlfriend. He cruises around town in a Bentley and lives in a large house on Webster Lake.

"Dirty Art" Freedman went on to run a saloon as well as a light bulb store. He retired at fifty-eight. Having hunted and fished, as far away as Wyoming and Alaska, he has slowed down since he had his shoulder and knee replaced. But he still lives on Cranberry Meadow Pond, where he claims he can catch a half dozen bass off his front porch when Ricky joins him.

* * *

In 1968, after serving in the Army Reserve, I moved to New York City and took the bar exam in 1971. I started my own law practice in 1972.

Although I was married, my wife and I never had children, which had been my dream. I had a major hand in raising my stepdaughter, Starlite Randall. But I always wanted a son and thought about it from the time I was very young, unhappy, in many respects, about the way I was raised. My parents gave me token glances here and there when I was shooting jump shots in the driveway. But when I played team sports, I seldom saw my dad on the sidelines. He was loving and kind, but we never talked as much as we should have. My mother and I talked about everything under the sun, but we didn't always see eye to eye. Her mood swings were catastrophic.

When I was sixty-two, I'd had enough of all the debris and jerks in my life and arranged to have a kid of my own through a surrogacy. It was a complex process. My son, Darrow, was born in 2007. He has changed my thinking about the purpose of my life. Now fifteen, he's wildly creative and plays five instruments. In 2018, for six months, he appeared on Broadway in the musical *School of Rock.* He's also a highly ranked tennis player.

He's not nearly as out there as I was. He has established his own rules about the way he wants to live when he grows up. No doubt he will succeed. He has an organized view of family, raising children and unlike me, I have never heard him raise his voice or lose his temper. There are no Lindas in his life and, I hope, there will never be any, although he is going through the trials of hanging out with capricious girls in his high school class. Sound familiar? He's a generous, kind, intelligent, caring person who makes me proud every day. My dream came true to have a best friend; it was what I was searching for in these pages.

* * *

Phil Cornell wrote

Golub's equivalent of "Rosebud" is "Linda Paul." Just like that aspect of Kane's youth stuck with him for life, she, too, occupies an enduring part of his recollection. Golub and Welles are saying the same thing really, about the formative experiences of youth.

THE END

Made in the USA
Middletown, DE
13 May 2023

30143794R00154